THE ORGANIZATIONAL SURVIVAL CODE

Designing Your Organization
To Get the Results You Want

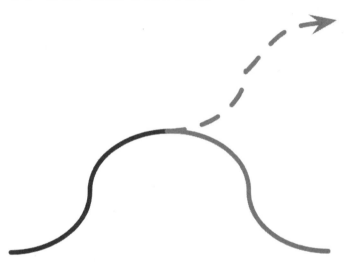

David P. Hanna

ISBN: 0615718515
ISBN-13: 9780615718514

Library of Congress Control Number: 2012952332
Hanoka Publishing
Mapleton, Utah

ADVANCE PRAISE FOR
THE ORGANIZATIONAL SURVIVAL CODE

professional experience to subjects such as organizational purpose, stakeholder alignment and process optimization. It combines practical checklists with down-to-earth change management analysis – definitely a compelling read."
  – Peter Vrijsen, Chief Human Resources Officer, Cargill Inc.

"Dave Hanna draws from a lifetime of experience and insight to provide us with a simple roadmap for keeping our organization on top. He includes some of the best real world examples to illustrate that organizations can adapt to survive and thrive. Better yet, he paints a vision of our highest organizational aspirations: people growth and doing good in the world. The book is authentic and genuine, as is its author."
  – Brad Taylor, Vice President, Human Resources, General Mills, Inc.

"This book captures simple, time tested practices and philosophies that drive success in a variety of contexts. Whether you are leading in your home, community, or business, *The Organizational Survival Code* applies."
  – Sean Morrison, Global HR Leader for Corporate Function Design, Procter & Gamble

"Tremendous! Dave Hanna delivers again, this time with a brilliant and insightful book about how to get and stay organizationally fit in a fast-changing world. *The Organizational*

Survival Code provides the strategies and tools needed not only to get to the top of the mountain, but most importantly, to stay there. I highly recommend this book—you'll find it engaging, relevant and immediately actionable."
– Stephen M. R. Covey, Author of *The New York Times* and
1 *Wall Street Journal* bestseller, *The Speed of Trust*,
and Coauthor of *Smart Trust*

"With his latest book, Dave Hanna provides very useful and practical guidelines for business partners, enabling us to examine organizational structures critically within a complex global context and then to modify and adjust them for economic survival. Know-how and practices for diagnosis, strategy and reorganization are imparted in a simple, efficient, and effective way. By using biological references and concrete examples, Hanna creates a vivid and heartening image of how sustainable survival will be feasible."
– Ursula Schütze-Kreilkamp, Head of Group HR Development
and Group Executives, Deutsche Bahn AG

"Dave Hanna has done us a great service in his new book. He explains with clarity and illuminating examples why most organizations don't survive and how they can avoid that fate. Indeed, he provides us with a fundamental framework along with step-by-step processes and tools to redesign organizations so that they not only survive but thrive. This is an important resource to help troubled organizations rebound and thriving organizations avoid becoming obsolete."

–Alan Wilkins, Professor, Organizational Leadership & Strategy, Brigham Young University

"Once again Dave Hanna has delivered an excellent book on how to improve business performance. The book mixes competent management advice with a variety of practical examples and is a must on the reading list for leaders at any level."

– Stella-Rosa Klöppner, head of executive development, REWE Group

"With the Organizational Survival Code, Dave Hanna provides elegant, straightforward guidance on how to build organizations that will thrive in the midst of complexity and constant change. This is a superb handbook for leaders who are determined to ensure their firms are fit for the future."

– Julie Staudenmier, Executive Director, Global Pharamaceutical Firm

TABLE OF CONTENTS

PREFACE

The economic recession, that hit us all in the closing days of 2008 and continues beyond the publishing of this book, has disrupted many a financial plan and business strategy. Companies everywhere have struggled to find firm footing in the new conditions. Many of their associates have had to "downsize" their standard of living in the process. None of this should have surprised any of us. We all know that economies cycle up and down, but in our hearts in 2008, we hoped the latest down cycle wouldn't come when it did.

Just as economies cycle up and down, so do organizational patterns of strategizing, operating, innovating, and responding to economic cycles. Study these patterns closely enough, and you will see that an organization's performance and the results it delivers are not shaped by coincidences. Patterns in human organizations are indicative of some design: those decisions to do X instead of Y; to continue doing A even after B has outperformed it for some time. Organizational patterns are shaped by the confluence of people, processes, systems, and culture. An organization's longevity is determined by the alignment of its patterns with what's going on in today's marketplace.

That marketplace is now a global one. Its requirements squeeze some players out of the game. It causes some of yesterday's star performers to become mediocre. It also provides opportunities to break out of the old mold and rise to a new level of success.

This book aims to help you seize the opportunities before you and stay on an upward path.

The good news is that organizational patterns can be reshaped by their stewards. This means your organization's destiny lies in your own hands. In the words of my good friend, Arthur Jones, "All organizations are perfectly designed to get the results they get." Put another way, every good and bad result your organization now delivers is the product of some designed patterns. You can redesign these patterns – reshape them, discard them, invent new ones. The counsel of this book is to redesign your organizational patterns based on a code of conduct that has been in evidence all around us for centuries.

I call this code of conduct the Organizational Survival Code, a set of seven capabilities that enable an organization to survive and even thrive through fitful economic cycles, changing market preferences, and the emergence of new technologies. The seven organizational capabilities are human applications of ecological principles that have enabled natural ecosystems to exist for centuries. The many examples provided here may help you understand that major organizational successes and downfalls both are explained by adherence to or violation of the Code.

Align with the Code to employ the right organizational patterns to stay at the top of your game – regardless of changes and transformations that are yet to come.

ACKNOWLEDGEMENTS

If it takes a village to raise a child, what kind of community does it take to educate someone to write about organizational survival in today's volatile and increasingly complex global marketplace? I have been the beneficiary of teachers, mentors, and friends from many backgrounds who have shaped my framework of the world and the organizations who strive to excel in it.

The Marriott Graduate School of Business at Brigham Young University (especially the founders of the organizational behavior program, Bill Dyer and Weldon Moffitt), introduced me to the world of organizations. Bill and Weldon recruited well and added Bonner Ritchie, Gene Dalton, Paul Thompson, Stephen Covey, David Cherrington, and a host of others to the faculty. In the past five decades the influence of this program has grown from three graduate students in the initial class to an alumni force of several hundred that literally influences people in all corners of the world today.

Managers and colleagues of the Procter & Gamble Company built on my early academic training and brought theory to life through the work we did. My first mentor, Herb Stokes, helped me and many others understand scientific principles of open systems theory and organization design and apply them in remarkable ways. Laurence Megson, Dennis King, Craig Decker, Ken Richardson, Doris Holzheimer, Arthur Jones, Holger Krug, Mike Crowther, Judy Palmer, and James Allsop patiently brought me along to a better understanding of how sound theory made for better practice.

Almost hidden among the many valuable products and services produced by the Covey Leadership Center was the organizational thinking of Jim Stuart, Blaine Lee, Roger Merrill, Jeff Call, and Stephen M.R. Covey, who all helped me build a bridge between leadership and organization design.

My colleagues at the RBL Group, primarily Dave Ulrich, Norm Smallwood, Mark Nyman, Ernesto Uscher, Starr Eckholdt, and Joe Hanson, have opened my eyes to the pure business sense delivered by the way an organization is designed.

And then there are the many clients who have applied and magnified whatever tools and approaches I had to offer them: most notably Procter & Gamble's John Feldmann, Wayne Richards, Frank Myerscough, Uwe Spiecker, and John Pepper; Ritz-Carlton's Horst Schulze, Beverly Enterprises' Boyd Hendrickson, S.C. Johnson's Ray Johnson, Hoffmann La Roche's Eduard Holdener, LOOP's CaSandra Cooper-Gates and Tom Shaw, Krasny Proletary's Yuri and Lena Kirillov and

Maxim Illin, Shell's Jim Funk, Metro Cash & Carry's Peter Vrijsen and Stella-Rosa Klöppner, Raytheon's Jon Jones, and Saturn's Skip LeFauve and Gary High.

Just as no village can fully compensate for a child's poor home life, all of these wonderful mentors might have been wasted if it weren't for my wife and best friend, Charlee. She has been much more than a mere traveling companion on my many journeys. She is the one who (lovingly!) has provoked me through the years to stretch to make a greater contribution to our society. She is a leader who personally has sacrificed much for family, business, and community. I have learned much from her example and counsel.

Finally, I am grateful for Jane Davis, who not only edited the manuscript, but also brought greater focus and clarity to some of the key concepts through her questions and comments. She is definitely the best editor I have ever worked with.

The book you hold in your hands is the legacy of all these wonderful mentors and tangible proof that, especially for those who have already passed from this life, a teacher's influence survives and even thrives in changing times.

Dave Hanna

Mapleton, Utah

PART ONE:
Organizations as Endangered Species

1
Survival by Design

"Whatever can be done, will be done. If not by incumbents, it will be done by emerging players. If not in a regulated industry, it will be done in a new industry born without regulation. Technological change and its effects are inevitable. Stopping them is not an option."

—*ANDY GROVE*

"If it weren't for the people..." said Finnerty, "always getting tangled up in the machinery. If it weren't for them, the world would be an engineer's paradise."

—*KURT VONNEGUT, PLAYER PIANO*

Many organizations are on the endangered species list in the 21st century. To be sure, there are opportunities everywhere. Companies today can communicate instantly with businesses on other continents as though they were just down the street. Emerging technology provides the means to deliver countless new products and services. All of these opportunities entice competitors to "seize the day."

At the same time, keeping up in this global, competitive race has never been harder. Customer expectations climb higher with each new product innovation. Product lifecycles are incredibly short. Many of today's successful products will be obsolete within months of their market debut. Customer service can be faster, more effective, and performed from any geographical location – thanks to the Internet.

Keeping your company healthy in this "best-of-times, worst-of-times" marketplace is a formidable challenge. Whoever is able to meet the market's needs better, faster, and cheaper than others will get plenty of business. Those who are not able to do this will be pushed aside. Thus, many organizations are on the endangered species list.

Here are some typical situations that threaten an organization's survival:

- **The worldwide economic turndown deals a serious blow to Liz's business.** She had planned to introduce two new products into the market before the economic indicators began their downward plunge. Now money is scarce, budgets are being revised and expenditures for anything beyond "the basics" are being cancelled. "How can we stretch our budget money to cover these new product intros?" Liz asked her leadership team. Doing more with less is not just a buzzword now, but an imperative for building her business.

- **Hal was an HR manager in charge of his company's talent management processes.** For several months he had been the target of complaints from the client groups he serviced. "They say I'm not filling their open slots fast enough," said Hal, "but I am doing the best I can with the staffing and the budget the company has given us. How can they expect me to do more?"

- **Kristen was a newly appointed global brand manager in a consumer products giant.** Senior management felt concern that the brand did not have a true global identity and was perceived very differently by customers in Asia, Europe, Africa, the Middle East, North America, and South America. Kristen was charged with developing a global brand strategy and re-launching the brand worldwide. "How do I get my colleagues in the different regions to even consider the possibility of a global brand strategy?" she asked. "All they talk about is how different their culture is from the other regions."

- **A flurry of recent acquisitions meant that Pat's company now had five product divisions instead of two.** Pat's IT group was expected to give the same level of service to the new divisions as it had provided for the established divisions. "We have retained some of the IT resources in the acquired companies," Pat said, "but not enough to cover all their needs. I've got to find a way to provide the same services to everyone with our present staffing."

■ **"It takes too long to get substantial forward movement in our company,"** admitted Stanley, chief financial officer for a large oil company. "We have so many departmental and geographical silos that we have to go through umpteen checkpoints to get agreement on a new financial reporting format. Our system shouldn't require this much time and energy."

Dilemmas Emerge from Organizational Misalignments

Managers everywhere face serious business dilemmas in today's business world. Virtually all dilemmas require some adjustment to strategy, processes, structure, systems, and behaviors to achieve optimal business results. This is precisely the work of organization design.

The purpose of this book is to help business partners successfully design their organizations to get the results they want–despite global complexities, stiff competition and rapidly changing economic cycles. My aim is to provide business leaders and HR professionals with some skills and state of the art tools for addressing their organizational dilemmas.

What I offer here is a framework and a set of principles and approaches that have helped many companies redesign themselves and regain their competitive momentum. These offerings can help you and your colleagues reshape how you work so that your company can *survive and even thrive* through the never-ending ups and downs of market cycles.

The Intangibles of Market Value

As we begin our exploration of designing organizations, we need to take note of an intriguing phenomenon has been shaping the marketplace over the past several decades. Whereas market value was once determined almost exclusively by bottom-line results and tangible assets, today it is being driven largely by what Professor Baruch Lev of NYU calls "intangibles." Intangibles are things like innovation, brand image, quality of leadership, a compelling strategy, and organizational capabilities. Consider this graph:

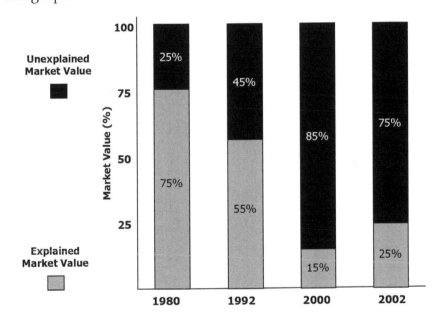

(Baruch Lev, *Intangibles: Management, Measurement and Reporting,* Brookings Institute Press, 2001)

As you can see here, factors that represent unexplained market value (e.g., intangibles) have grown to be a dominant factor influencing a corporation's market value. Analysts more and more are scrutinizing profitability, strategy, efficiencies, individual competencies, organizational structure and capabilities, and culture when evaluating the market value of a firm. One way of depicting these intangibles is this staircase:

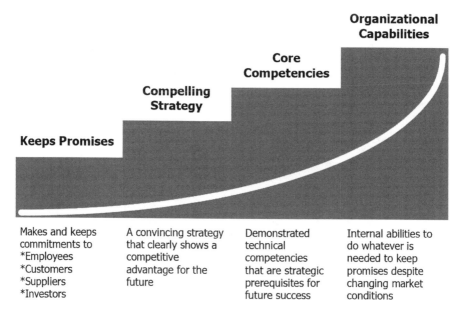

| Makes and keeps commitments to *Employees *Customers *Suppliers *Investors | A convincing strategy that clearly shows a competitive advantage for the future | Demonstrated technical competencies that are strategic prerequisites for future success | Internal abilities to do whatever is needed to keep promises despite changing market conditions |

Keeping promises to all stakeholders, formulating a compelling strategy, possessing the core competencies to deliver products and services to the marketplace, and having the organizational capabilities to mobilize the human resources to deliver everything else are key "intangibles" for any corporation.

Many managers are becoming fluent in reading this scorecard of intangibles and wish to lead the way in using them to improve their results. These managers need some resources that can add value beyond conventional managerial wisdom. They need to see and understand more of what goes on in complex organizations. They need a practical way to harness intangibles that will improve the bottom line.

Now is the time for managers and HR professionals to step up to the survival challenge. Those who demonstrate the following competencies will become leaders who enable their organizations to survive – and thrive – in today's challenging world.

- **The Competency to Diagnose:** the ability to see what others may miss in how the organization is really operating and to identify the multiple cause and effect streams that affect the bottom line.

- **The Competency to Apply Organization Theory:** an understanding of the theories, research findings and practical experience that can predict how people will work together in a variety of situations and the ability to apply this understanding in a practical way that delivers improved results.

- **The Competency to Design Highly Effective Organizations:** knowing the results of past experiments with organizational form in motivating and regulating work interactions so that reshaping strategy, processes, systems and structures produces optimal results.

As you can see, there is much significant theory, research, and practice in the field of organization design. What I will present in this book are a few time-tested principles and approaches that will enable your organization to move forward in the good and bad times that lie ahead.

2
Organizational Lifecycles

"There is the Moral of all human tales;
'Tis but the same rehearsal of the past.
First Freedom, and then Glory—when that fails,
Wealth, vice, corruption—barbarism at last.
And History, with all her volumes vast,
Hath but one page."

—LORD BYRON

Before we get into the tools and technology of organization design, let's step back and look at the bigger picture of organization effectiveness and survival. The big picture reveals a framework and some principles to keep the organization designer focused on the ultimate goal of survival.

As we consider the big picture, think about what the following companies have in common:

- Cambria Steel
- Guggenheim Exploration
- Lehigh and Wilkes-Barre Coal
- Intercontinental Rubber
- Schwarzchild and Sulzberger
- Central Leather

Each of these institutions was one of the top 100 U.S. firms in 1909[1], but none exists today as an independent entity. They are either out of business or a very minor player in some larger corporation. Some were quite large in their glory days (Central Leather was *number seven* on the 1909 list). Unfortunately they were not able to maintain their success. Within a few management generations, they have disappeared. These six are certainly not unusual: of the top 100 U.S. industrial firms in 1909, only 14 are still in the elite group today. Only 23 are still around at all!

To update this picture, I considered today's Fortune Top 100 list. I looked at global companies, not just those in the USA. The resulting table is most instructive:

---

[1]   A. D. H. Kaplan study in *Big enterprise in a competitive system*, Brookings Institution, 1954.

FORTUNE'S TOP 100 GLOBAL COMPANIES

2011 LEADERS	CASUALTIES OF THE 2000S
Wal-Mart (1)	Mitsubishi
Royal Dutch Shell (2)	Boeing
Exxon Mobil (3)	Credit Suisse
BP (4)	Unilever
Sinopec Group (5)	Sears Roebuck
Volkswagen (13)	DuPont
Carrefour (32)	Philips Electronics
McKesson (37)	Hypovereinsbank
Nestlé (42)	Enron
Procter & Gamble (80)	Bayer
Royal Bank of Scotland (100)	Motorola

The left column lists some representative leaders in the Global 100. The right column identifies some well-known companies who fell off of the list during the decade of the 2000s. These companies were not alone. In fact, 55 of the Top 100 fell off the list during the 2000s. Going back to the original list of 1909, a review of the Top 100 during the decade 1909-1919 shows 41 of those companies fell off the list, so regardless of the era, staying on top of the pack is hard to do. No doubt, many of the organizations who have slipped also have been busily engaged re-strategizing and redesigning some aspects of their operation. But, what good is *any* organization design if the organization itself fails to maintain its competitive advantage?

Consider further the reasons the companies fell off the list from 1909-1919:

- Changing economic conditions
- Mergers and acquisitions
- Emergence of new technologies

So what has changed in 100 years? Not much. Roughly 50 percent of the Top 100 fall within 10 years for the same fundamental reasons. This common pattern for the past century indicates there are some systemic forces at play, not just a series of coincidences or random events.

The struggle for life isn't peculiar to large corporations. The Office of Advocacy of the U.S. Small Business Administration (SBA) reports that 99.8 percent of new employer establishments are small firms. The Bureau of the Census report for the SBA indicates 70 percent of new firms survive two years, 50 percent survive five years, but only 33 percent survive 10 years. Hence my statement in Chapter 1, that many organizations are on the endangered species list.

Organizational Lifecycles

The common pattern from the Top 100 research and the SBA findings is illustrated by this lifecycle graphic. Though one organization may extend its peak phase longer than others, over time, most organizations' bottom line looks like this familiar bell-shaped curve:

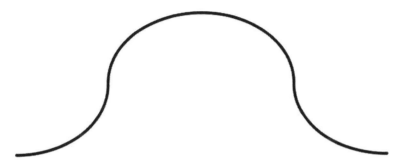

The lifecycle tells us that whenever people come together, certain dynamics tend to emerge. They unite themselves and grow, and then something happens and their unity begins to break down. Yet organizations are the only living systems that have the potential to live on indefinitely. They don't have to follow the up-and-down slope of the lifecycle.

In order to know how to extend an organization's lifecycle, we first need to understand its dynamics. What accompanies an organization's rise to peak performance? What drags it down? What must leaders keep in mind if they are to stand the test of time? To answer these questions, let's consider two organizational applications—the lifecycles of civilizations and product innovations. Both are extremely relevant to our present society and global economy. My intent in reviewing these lifecycles is not to make you a social anthropologist or research scientist. Examining their common patterns can help us better understand the natural laws and principles that govern both the ascent and descent of complex organizations.

What follows is a summary of thousands of years of human experience as documented by renowned historians. As you read this material, see if you can determine why, as Arnold Toynbee said, "Nothing fails like success."

Lifecycles of Civilizations

The world's great civilizations, such as Sumeria, Egypt, India, Greece, Rome, China, and Mesoamerica, all share a common lifecycle: they started from almost nothing, flourished, declined, and then either disappeared or lingered on as shadows of their former selves when others overtook them. German historian,

Robert Münzel, summed it up best, "Great nations rise and fall—the people go from bondage to spiritual faith, from spiritual faith to great courage, from courage to liberty, from liberty to abundance, from abundance to selfishness, from selfishness to complacency, from complacency to apathy, from apathy to dependency, from dependency back again into bondage." Building on this description, I offer this lifecycle with the following nine stages:

1. **Bondage:** most great civilizations start in bondage to others and either overthrow another group or emigrate to a new home. One key to moving out of bondage is tribal loyalty. The tribe is one, characterized by a shared sense of duty.

2. **Faith:** religious faith has accompanied the early rise of each civilization. The element of faith provides an overarching value system to which individual desires are subordinated.

3. **Courage:** all members courageously pursue the group's objectives to protect themselves from enemies and to expand their culture.

4. **Community:** city-states often expand the tribal loyalty to ever-wider circles of followers. Common values make citizenship a personal and fulfilling experience even as the population grows.

5. **Abundance:** each great civilization reaches a point where it becomes the envy of its neighbors. Abundance means there is plenty for everyone; that the quality of life is high for most people and not artificially constrained by social class.

6. **Selfishness:** the overarching set of values dissipates, enabling the people to glorify themselves and gratify their own desires. Divisions in beliefs and wealth become more pronounced. Cooperation breaks down.

7. **Greed:** the quest for self-gratification leads to greater materialism and an ever-increasing escalation of exploiting

other groups for the benefit of a select few. Said historian Charles H. Brough, *"Wealth corrupts, not immediately, but invariably."*

8. **Dependence:** inequality grows with greed, bringing a division between an advantaged minority and a deprived majority. Ironically, the civilization becomes dependent on its weakest link (deprived majority) for further progress.

9. **Bondage:** weakened civilizations eventually give way to other groups, thus the lifecycle comes full circle – from bondage to bondage, or in Byron's words, "a rehearsal of the past."

From the writings of Will and Ariel Durant, Emile Durkheim, Neville Kirk, Albert Schweitzer, Adam Seligman, Pitirim A. Sorokin, Oswald Spengler, Alexis de Tocqueville, Arnold Toynbee, and George M. Wrong emerge the following characteristics of a declining civilization:

- A declining sense of community and national pride (evidenced by political apathy) as people become more concerned with only their own private affairs
- A preponderance of great cities
- A worship of money and material wealth
- Religious values replaced by disparate and contending secular values and a resulting moral confusion

■ A lack of emphasis on the family, marriage, and the proper training of children, leading to further moral and social fragmentation

■ The rise of dictators

■ A cumulative weakness and chaos in the social fabric that leaves the population open to exploitation and/or decimation

The dynamics of this civilization lifecycle are profound because they transcend individual people, cultures, and even epochs of time. Every civilization is in fact an organization—a group of people working toward some common purpose over time. Pause for a moment and think of your organization as if it were one of the great civilizations. At which point in this lifecycle does your organization find itself? Are you ascending, on top, or sliding downhill? Do these attributes describe where your culture has come from, where it is now, or where the current trends will lead you?

The Product Lifecycle

The civilization lifecycle closely resembles another lifecycle—that of the product innovation process. The rise and fall of today's industrial organizations are due to dynamics that are very similar to those of civilizations. The lifecycle of developing innovative goods and services looks like this:

1. **Debt:** The initial context for all innovations is debt, meaning they are dependent on other organizational resources for their sponsorship and execution.

2. **Vision:** Every innovation is sparked by a vision of a better solution (product, technology, or service) to someone's need. The computer and overnight courier services both began as some individual's vision of a better world.

3. **Persistence:** Persistence is required by the innovator (often referred to as a product champion) to move from vision to reality against a tide of opposition from the status quo.

4. **Divergence:** This stage calls for experimentation to test the validity of the concept by exploring different alternatives without prematurely judging any as "good" or "bad."

5. **Convergence:** Out of the many options previously explored, a single prototype is selected to introduce into the market place. Now all of the organization's departments must converge for the product launch.

6. **Market Share:** A period of growth. The market evaluates the new innovation and determines its relative value compared to other available offerings. Abundance follows when the desired market share is realized.

7. **Inward Focus:** Prosperity brings with it a greater emphasis on internal issues such as production costs, economies of scale and standardization to minimize expansion costs and stabilize the product's quality and reliability.

8. **Win-Lose Strategy:** As others imitate the new innovation, the focus subtly drifts toward the competitive battle and away from the customer. Win-Lose strategies emerge, attempting to maximize self-interests vs. competition.

9. **Follow Competition:** The inward focus, at a time when competing products are introduced and consumer expectations are being reshaped, results in a loss of the competitive edge. The innovator now becomes a follower.

10. **Out of Business:** The product dies or is replaced by a newer form. This newer form may come from within its own organization or from competition.

Think of how we got the light bulb, penicillin, the newest electronic invention, and countless other items that contribute to our standard of living. In each case, product lifecycle dynamics have been evident. Think further about companies, products or services that have become obsolete. Again, the lifecycle has been conspicuous as carriages gave way to automobiles, phonograph records were largely replaced by compact discs and mp3s, and conventional mail services were displaced largely by fax technology and the internet.

Again I invite you to place your own product or service where you think it fits today on the product lifecycle. Are you just approaching the desired market share, already at the top, or falling from where you used to be?

Consider for a moment the common threads revealed in these two lifecycles—and what lessons you can apply to your own situation:

The similarities are striking and pose some serious questions. Why is it that with all our technical advances, with our unparalleled capacity to learn and store knowledge, with the coming of reengineering, balanced scorecards, quality and reliability management, and sophisticated strategic planning methods—why is it with all this going for us we are unable to build organizations that can hold up over time? One wonders if any system can survive more than a few decades…

There is a light at the end of this tunnel. Organizations do have the potential to "jump the curve" and avoid the downward plunge. In the next chapter, I will explore the other half of the big picture—the survival code that will enable your organization to break out of the lifecycle's fatal path.

3
The Organizational Survival Code

"Grandfather so often told me I should take all things to the temples of Creation to test them out. If they are real, if they are true for everyone, if they are simple, then they are a universal truth. If these things are tested in Creation and do not work, then they should be abandoned, because they then are the workings of (someone's) overactive imagination."

—*TOM BROWN, JR.*

In the previous chapter I raised the disturbing notion that organizations are fragile institutions. Even the biggest and best have a very hard time hanging on to their position in the marketplace. Thousands of smaller organizations will tell you the market doesn't play favorites with them either. You either produce what the market values or you begin to fade from view. But there is hope. Our examination of the big picture needs to consider those systems that have lasted for ages and the natural laws that govern their survival.

The most enduring systems are found in nature. The oldest tree on this planet is a spruce discovered in the mountainous Dalarna province of Sweden.[2] This tree is estimated to be 9,550 years old. Ecosystems of mountains, forests, streams and meadows are amazingly resilient. These systems can survive physical calamities, destructive weather patterns and other major environmental shifts and endure for ages unless humans intervene and attempt to "civilize" them. What these natural systems have in common with civilizations and product organizations is that they are all *living* systems, meaning some of their key elements are living, breathing entities. A review of the natural laws that govern the survival of living systems offers profound wisdom for understanding organizational longevity.

Natural Laws

Let me take a moment to elaborate on the concept of a natural law. A natural law expresses a universal truth that governs the makeup of something or some dynamic process. An example from the world of physics is the natural law of gravity. Jump off a cliff and you will fall to the ground below. Natural laws are not subject to our desires or beliefs; we are

2   Umeå University (2008, April 16). World's oldest living tree -- 9550 years old --discovered in Sweden. *ScienceDaily.*

always subject to their rules. In other words, *natural laws govern our interactions whether or not we are aware of them, agree with them, or follow them.* We must align ourselves with these laws to arrive—and remain—in a desirable place.

But how do we know if something is truly a natural law, or merely someone's value or preference? A practical way to determine the difference is to *look at the universality and timelessness of the value.* If the value leads to success in a wide variety of circumstances, in diverse cultures, in all ages, then it qualifies as a natural law. Individual preferences, on the other hand, may serve us well in some specific situations, but not in others.

Because the following seven attributes are always present in living systems that survive over time, I believe they qualify as natural laws.

1. **Ecological order**: *each element of the ecosystem must fit into the order of things.* Living systems are all part of a larger network of elements. They either fit into this ecosystem in a way that maintains balance of the greater whole, or they perish.

2. **Purpose**: *everything else is subordinated to the highest purpose— survival for self, group and species.* Natural instincts lead to self-preservation, the law of the pack, and preservation of the species. Failure to be concerned with anything beyond self ultimately leads to ecological imbalance and death.

3. **Steady state**: *survival is maintained via steady processes that follow a proven, functional routine.* The steady state is a

pattern of habits that assures daily survival and stores energy for meeting critical challenges. Without a steady state, the system uses more energy than it can obtain from the environment.

4. **Mobilization**: *threats to the steady state are sensed and met.* The dynamic of mobilization is a two-edged sword. It certainly protects the steady state. On the other hand, it could actually repel a force for change that would be necessary for survival. Mobilization resists *all* attempts to disrupt the steady state.

5. **Complexity**: *systems develop more complex, specialized functions.* In nature, greater complexity generally leads to *expanding* skills or functions and a *greater ability to adapt* to the environment. In human organizations, greater complexity usually translates into creating *steeper* hierarchies and *narrower* spans of control.

6. **Synergy**: *the whole is greater than the sum of its parts.* Synergy doesn't come from simply assembling more elements; it comes from establishing new relationships among those elements. Bringing together diverse elements in new ways is the creative force that shapes the survival of both a species and an organization.

7. **Adaptation**: *processes change as necessary when environmental changes threaten survival.* Effective living systems subordinate processes to purpose. They are able to grow and adapt in remarkable ways when new environmental conditions require them to do so.

These seven natural laws govern all living systems—from single elements like sagebrush and bison, to complex systems like forests and human organizations. They identify for us the capabilities an organization must possess if it would endure for more than a few decades. Now consider how these natural laws fit into the lifecycle patterns I have already reviewed. Adhering to these laws explains the ascent up the lifecycle and violating them explains why organizations fall from their peak.

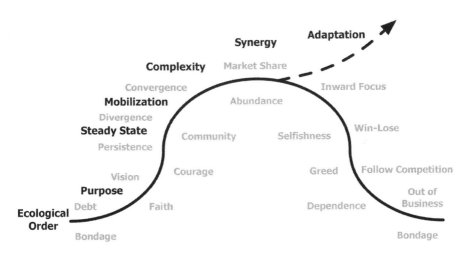

Any organization must fit into the **ecological order** of the marketplace if it is to have the roots for growth and prosperity. Though the organization starts out in debt and "bondage," it can fit into the market ecology if it fills important needs. The organization's initial challenges are to develop a compelling, common **purpose**, develop a **steady-state** operation that fulfills this purpose, and **mobilize** all its resources to deliver the steady state. Successful growth challenges the capacity of the new organization and requires greater **complexity** (e.g., greater functionality) to maintain its performance. When everything comes together successfully, there is a sense of community between the organization and its stakeholders, and **synergy** emerges, resulting in an abundant market share. But the challenges of change are constant, therefore, the length of the lifecycle ultimately is tied to the organization's ability to further **adapt** to an ever-advancing environment.

The fragile nature of organizations comes from the fact that they are most often shaped by human policies. To the degree their policies adhere to the natural laws described here, the organization's longevity is enhanced, but if the policies conflict with natural laws, the system's lifecycle will be shortened. (I will examine some of these human organizational policies in more detail in chapter 8.)

As the lifecycle reviews have already demonstrated, most organizations fall from their peak because instead of staying aligned with natural laws, they become internally focused and fall **out of the ecological order** that sustains their livelihood. At the very point when the competitive market is stimulated to produce something new, the organization suffers from internal myopia: a fixation on internal needs rather than market needs. Greed and win-lose obsessions (both self-serving) become **counterfeits for purpose** (I don't know many people who would willingly sacrifice their own well-being for someone else's greed). In an attempt to further standardize and control the steady state, **human complexity** (i.e., bureaucratic supervision) substitutes for natural complexity (greater adaptability), further focusing everyone's attention only on their piece of the whole. The more fragmented the system's elements become, the more dependent they are on factors outside their control when attempting to make meaningful improvements. The bottom line of all this is that the instincts for further adaptation are blunted and the organization accelerates down the path of obsolescence.

The Organizational Survival Code

The conclusion to be drawn from the previous section is straightforward: *you must adhere to the natural laws of living systems if you would continuously extend your organization's lifecycle.* It is straightforward, but certainly not easy to do! Here is the survival code for the organization in the 21st century that follows nature's script:

1. **Ecological Order:** Strategize to fulfill the most important needs and expectations of your key stakeholders.
2. **Purpose:** Develop a compelling purpose and strategy so that each member instinctively acts to fulfill it.
3. **Steady State:** Design work processes that consistently deliver high quality outputs.
4. **Mobilization:** Solve problems at their source.
5. **Complexity:** Empower more self-sufficient, flexible, multi-skilled people and work units.
6. **Synergy:** Develop true partnerships with all stakeholders to always enjoy a competitive advantage.
7. **Adaptation:** Re-strategize and redeploy resources in the midst of external changes to stay atop the lifecycle.

If these characteristics were typical of the way your corporation conducted itself, your lifecycle would look like this:

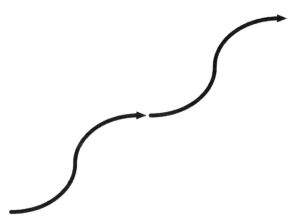

This is the famous S-Curve, as it is known in the field of research and product development. It is the curve that illustrates how a product (or the producing organization) may leap beyond the traditional lifecycle and renew life in a market environment that itself is always advancing. The critical point is in the vicinity of the first arrow. If the organization were able to adapt at the peak of abundance and refocus on ecological order and purpose instead of being blinded by internal myopia, the lifecycle would begin a new upward spiral instead of sliding down. It is the capacity for continuous improvement and adaptation that critically influences corporate longevity. Some corporate examples:

■ In 1837, William Procter, a candle maker, and James Gamble, a soap maker, joined forces to create the Procter & Gamble company. Through the years, P&G's commitment to delivering top quality products has fueled its evolution to becoming one of the top 100 global companies in Fortune Magazine's Global 500 rankings. P&G's stable of branded products has a storied history of innovation and accomplishment. Along the way, however, P&G has expanded into product lines never envisioned by its founders: food and beverages, paper products, health care, beauty care, pet foods, and shaving products. It has faced a number of dilemmas along the way. For instance, what do you do with superior products (in test markets) that can't sustain themselves against strongly-entrenched competitors? Or, what do you do with market leaders that no longer meet changing consumer needs? P&G has painfully, but correctly, sold off such sentimental product favorites as Crisco shortening, Jif peanut butter, Folgers coffee and Pringles potato chips when market research indicated these would no longer justify future investment of time and resources. P&G's growth, nonetheless, has continued. In the past decade the company's number of billion dollar brands has doubled from 10 to 20.

■ Apple Inc. began in the mid '70s as Steve Jobs' and Steven Wozniak's vision of a personal computer. The two young men developed their first prototype in a home garage and went up against U.S. computer giant IBM when they launched their first computer on the market. The garage operation gave way to a state-of-the-art manufacturing process and Apple earned a small, but loyal segment of the market. The company has survived numerous ups and downs economically from 1976 to the present day. Its ability to collaborate and innovate has attracted committed associates who have developed a stable of leading-edge products (notebook computers, iPod portable music players, iPhones, iPads) to become the world's largest company based on market capitalization. Study the corporate evolution from Apple Computer to Apple Inc. and you will find the survival code elements all have played a role in its success. Much of Apple's fortunes have been attributed to founder Steve Jobs. We shall see if his successors are able to sustain Apple's success. Their adherence to the organizational survival code will be essential.

On the other hand, we have seen companies operate contrary to the survival code, succumb to the lifecycle dynamics and disappear after years of success.

- People Express, a pioneer in the budget airline segment, experienced a meteoric rise and fall in less than six years. It grew very rapidly, earning $1 billion in its fifth year and then going out of business the year after. Rapid growth, through expanding the number of airplanes and a merger with Frontier Airlines, destroyed the steady state. Flights were consistently overbooked, thousands of passenger bags were lost each month, and aircraft were poorly maintained. When senior managers voiced concern about how "too much growth too fast" was endangering their survival, CEO Don Burr dismissed their concerns and kept expanding. People Express' original value proposition to its customers (low fare regional flights) became blurred with focus on coast-to-coast and even international flights. The win-lose premise (expand today at all costs) ended a once-promising entrepreneurial concept. Violate the survival code and you will go down. Adhere to the survival code principles and you will survive and even thrive, as Southwest Airlines has proven.
- Eastman Kodak once was THE photography business, selling more than 80 percent of all cameras and film in the U.S.

for most of the 20th century. But competition came calling, and in the 1980s Fuji began to eat into Kodak's large market shares with lower priced films. The digital revolution began prototyping more sophisticated, easy-to-use cameras and simple, inexpensive photo processing. Kodak mobilized insufficient responses to the new competition. Though it first developed its own digital camera in 1975, company leadership couldn't imagine it replacing their traditional camera models. Past merger attempts to stimulate growth only drained cash from Kodak's coffers. It let go of its own home-grown Eastman Chemical business, today a thriving Fortune 500 company. A rigidity of purpose in changing times has prevented Kodak from reinventing itself like Procter & Gamble did. Kodak remains exclusively a photography company, even though the technology it has developed could be applied in new business arenas, such as social media. The one time industry giant is following far behind competition in the market it once dominated. Stock prices have plummeted in the past decade and the company is surrounded by rumors of bankruptcy.

As these examples show, the organizational survival code is not just a theoretical formula constructed in some ivory tower. It is real wisdom that comes from studying the big picture and actual market dynamics. In the following chapters I will focus on some practical tools and processes that can make this survival code a living force in your company.

4
How to Design to Code

---

*"All organizations are perfectly designed
to get the results they get."*

— *ARTHUR W. JONES*

---

*"Most ailing organizations have developed a functional blindness
to their own defects. They are not suffering because they cannot
resolve their problems but because they cannot see their problems."*

— *JOHN GARDNER*

The organizational survival code represents a standard to which a company may aspire. The lifecycles represent milestones that show us where we are vs. our standard. The hard work required to stay on top of the lifecycle begins with the work of organization design – shaping strategy, systems, attitudes and behaviors to do whatever it takes to align your particular organization with the code.

A common error in organization design approaches is to work on certain design pieces in isolation. Because of this flaw in approach, setting a strategy, adjusting the executive compensation system, revising hiring criteria, downsizing, outsourcing and similar approaches too often do not deliver the desired outcomes. In this chapter I will introduce a practical tool for diagnosing and designing your organization as a whole system. The processes of diagnosis and design can save you much wasted effort and frustration. The holistic picture of your organization will help you identify the few things you can do to have an enormous impact on your bottom line – and eventual survival. The following chapters will describe many tools and approaches that can be used to align with the survival code. But the decision about whether you should use any of these tools should be based on a big picture understanding of your organization and its stakeholder needs.

The Organizational Systems Model

The Organizational Systems Model (OSM) is a framework for keeping in perspective the big picture of key variables that impact organizational performance.

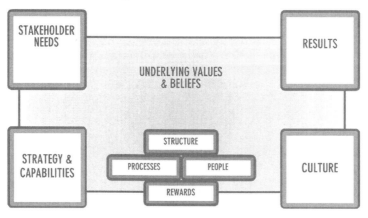

Indeed, the organization is a system that can appear to be complex and puzzling to those who manage it. Arthur Jones, a former colleague of mine at Procter & Gamble, first coined this phrase: "All organizations are perfectly designed to get the results they get." Think about this statement for a minute. What this means is every organization has ways of balancing out the many demands for its time, attention, resources and energy. Depending on the balance struck, the organization performs and delivers results. Think of this balancing act as "design." Design is not just structure. It is not always formal or conscious. This balancing of resources isn't always fixed—you may not do things the same way every time and your results may vary (even drastically!) from month to month. However, you can't really argue with this statement—the fact that certain results occur (and not others) verifies that *some design* has been perfectly executed.

The key point this process model illustrates is that organizational performance can be influenced by the degree to which critical elements harmonize. So what are these elements?

First, the **Stakeholder Needs** the organization must fulfill, such as:

- Shareholder expectations.
- Customer expectations of product quality and service.

- Supplier expectations around product, cost, timing, flexibility and trust.
- Employee expectations of income, challenging work, job security and personal growth.
- Community expectations concerning corporate citizenship, environmental responsibility, and social standards.

Identifying and meeting the most essential of these needs and expectations are the very keys of organizational survival.

The second element is the **Strategy & Capabilities**. The strategy sets the direction for what's important in the system. It may be expressed as a mission, vision, and/or strategy. It may also include more operational elements like operating principles, values, and goals. These define what things will be done and what things won't be done. They determine what the critical tasks of the organization will be. Organizational Capabilities are those intangibles that are required to fulfill the strategy. They include such things as efficiency, collaboration, leadership, strategic clarity, shared mindset, innovation, accountability, and customer connectivity. An accounting firm competing on a strategic platform of matchless customer service might require customer connectivity, shared mindset, and efficiency to be successful. The Strategy & Capabilities serve as design specifications to shape the specific organizational systems.

The third element is **Organizational Systems**. These are the organizational tools used to implement the Strategy and deliver the organizational capabilities. These systems include *Processes* (meaning work processes), *Structure* (how work is divided up and connected), *Rewards* (the incentives and consequences for either delivering or not delivering what the strategy and capabilities require), and *People* (including talent management systems and leadership competencies). These tools provide

structure to work tasks and reinforce patterns of behavior. They are the "glue" holding the culture in place. A key to consistent results is to ensure that all of these systems are aligned with one another.

Fourth, the **Culture** of the organization, or the work habits and norms that explain how the organization really operates. The way the system really operates is what produces results— whether they are good or bad.

Fifth, the actual **Results** being delivered currently. These results either fulfill or fall short of the stakeholder needs listed earlier.

Sixth, the **Underlying Values & Beliefs** of people in the organization. This includes the often-invisible elements such as individual values, beliefs and assumptions. These influence how all the other elements are viewed and designed. These beliefs also tell the system when changes are needed or that the status quo is okay.

These are the key elements that affect an organization's results. Now let's see what an organization diagnosis process looks like in this framework.

The Diagnosis Process

Why discuss organizational diagnosis in a book focused on organization design? Because the end prescription is only as good as the diagnosis that precedes it. Knowing what the organization must do to survive and understanding what is hindering it from doing so are both vital to prescribing the appropriate organization design that will truly make a difference in results.

All too often, managers and the consultants they employ believe they already know how the organization needs to be reconfigured to improve their results. They attack the problem by immediately making design changes. For example, some common reactions to poor results are to set new goals, or to modify the bonus system, or to restructure or to replace the manager. As managers and consultants have suggested such things in the past, I have asked them, "Have you ever tried this before?"

"Yes," is their frequent answer.

"Has this always produced better results?" is my next question.

"Well… no," is usually the embarrassed reply.

Prescribing without first diagnosing doesn't work any better for organizations than it does for purchasing your next pair of glasses or contact lenses. Well-intentioned but faulty prescriptions perpetuate what John Gardner referred to as "a functional blindness" to an organization's defects. Diagnosis is key to seeing what the real problems are.

We begin the diagnosis process with the top two boxes— Stakeholder Needs and Results–and proceed clockwise around the map.

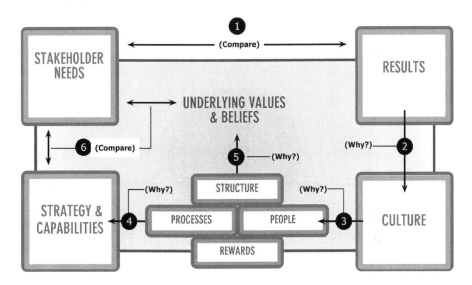

Step One. We compare the requirements of the Stakeholder Needs with the Results actually delivered at present. Given this comparison and extrapolating today's performance vs. evolving stakeholder needs, we can determine what needs to change and what needs to remain the same.

Step Two. Next we move down to Culture from Results. There are many definitions of culture in the literature today due to its particularly complex nature. Culture is much like air; it is everywhere we look and touches everything that goes on in organizations. It is both a cause and an effect of organizational behavior. The more we learn about organizations, the more elements of culture we discover. There are behaviors, values, assumptions, rites, rituals, folklore, heroes, creeds, physical artifacts, climate, etc. Unfortunately, the definitions of culture that are the most inclusive are also the most esoteric and unwieldy to the manager. They cause many managers to shrug at the prospect of ever understanding—or managing—culture.

I propose a more limited but pragmatic definition of culture to be used in the context of the OSM. When focusing on the culture box in the model, I prefer to think of culture as the observable work habits and practices that explain how the organization really operates. When viewed this way, culture is not some mystical phenomenon that has no relevance to effectiveness. On the contrary, it is a critical factor of organizational performance—and something every manager needs to understand. There is a "hidden" side of culture (underlying values and beliefs) that is included in the heart of the model because values, beliefs and assumptions are causal forces that shape many of the other system's dynamics.

These two elements, 1) the behaviors and work patterns one can observe and 2) the underlying values and beliefs, are generally regarded by most theorists as being core components of culture. Focusing on them simplifies things considerably. We can't fully understand everything about culture, but we can understand the essential behaviors and values, and these two areas have the most critical influence on results.

A cultural diagnosis is done by examining each result (good or bad) currently produced and asking the question "Why?" For instance, *why is profit satisfactory? Why is product quality below the acceptable level? Why is turnover rising in the last quarter?* To answer each of these questions, we identify the observable daily behaviors that logically explain the results. In the above example of unacceptable product quality, we might identify the following behaviors:

- Associates don't perform the quality checks using the standard process.
- The Quality department frequently changes the standard process.
- If production falls behind its commitments, everyone focuses on getting products shipped, not quality.

In the above example, do these behaviors give a logical explanation for the poor result? Will the result improve if these behaviors stay the same? This is the kind of connection we are looking for in Step Two.

Step Three. Having identified the cultural elements (behaviors) influencing results, we now move into the Organization Systems. The culture is largely determined by the quality of, and fit between, the *processes, structure, rewards,* and *people* systems. This diagnostic step takes each element of culture previously identified and asks why these cultural behaviors exist. The answers are then traced into each of the four organizational systems categories. Again, we can ask ourselves which of these design features we want to keep and which we want to change.

For example, let's say we are tracing the causes of an organizational culture in which people do whatever it takes to finish a project on time. Looking at the systems, we might find:

- People are organized into specific project teams. (Structure)
- Each project team has a weekly project review with top management to assure everyone that the project is on track. (Process)
- Those who don't meet deadlines don't move ahead career-wise in the company. (Rewards)
- The company has a reputation for hiring high achievers, usually in the top 10 percent of their graduating class. (People)

In this example, the four systems are perfectly designed to have people finish projects on time. The cause and effect connections look like this:

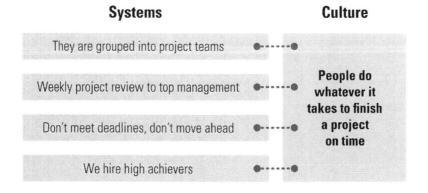

Step Four. We ask ourselves why the particular organizational systems have been chosen and/or perpetuated. This step looks at the formal Strategy & Capabilities for the cause of the cultural behaviors. Is there something in the mission, vision, strategy, values, or goals/objectives that explains the systems design choices? Is our strategy of "low cost producer" reflected in our organizational systems? Has the drive to establish the capabilities of engineering excellence and innovation shaped information systems around technical standards to the omission of employee opinions? There may be many or few connections between strategy & capabilities and systems. Make a note of whatever is evident or missing between the two, then move on to Step Five.

Step Five. This is where the deeper level of culture comes in. Frequently, organizational systems are chosen based on Underlying Values and Beliefs of people. To find out what these values, beliefs and assumptions are, we deduce them from the pattern of organizational systems, cultural behaviors, and results from the previous steps. For instance,

- If the **result** is an unacceptable cycle time, and
- The **culture** is one of people waiting for the boss to give orders and to always ask permission before acting, and
- The **organizational systems** show this behavior is rewarded and initiative without prior approval is punished.

What underlying value or belief would explain the whole dynamic? It might be something like, *"The boss knows best."*

These beliefs do not always correspond to the published or agreed-upon strategy, just as the organization's culture doesn't always match the formal organization chart. However, uncovering these underlying values is crucial, because any improvement you attempt to make will likely fail if these underlying elements are not addressed.

Step Six. We compare the Strategy/Capabilities and Underlying Values and Beliefs with the Stakeholder Needs and note areas of alignment or misalignment. It is at this point that many leaders understand they have become their own worst enemy. They recognize their beliefs have supported ineffective design choices that have sustained a culture that delivers today's poor results. (In the above example, the belief that *"the boss knows best"* is actually a driving force for *unacceptable cycle time*.) The good news is, I have seen some leaders willingly change their values and beliefs once they recognized these were self-defeating.

This completes the diagnosis process. We should now have a better understanding of why our results are exceptional or in need of improvement, and we should be clear about the elements that are helping or hindering our results.

The Design Process

Now let's examine the process of designing the organization to get the results you want.

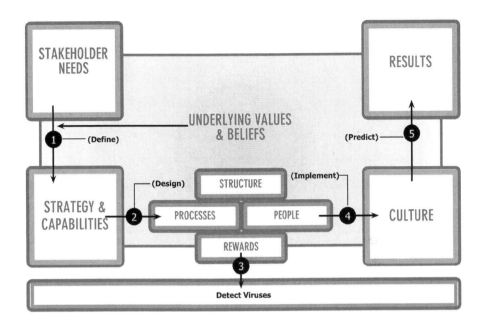

Step One. We start by defining the elements of Strategy/ Capabilities that align with the Stakeholder Needs.

This step considers the basic strategy of the organization (in the context of key stakeholder needs) by asking such questions as:

- What is our reason for being?
- What business are we in?
- How do we choose to compete in our businesses?
- What are our core technologies?

Many organizations also take time to get a clear sense of mission. Mission supplements the Strategy by identifying:

- The organization's distinctive competencies.

- The organization's unique contribution.
- How our life's desires can be expressed in our work.
- Our core values (or operating principles).

An important note to this last point on core values: this is a good opportunity to address some of the dysfunctional underlying values and beliefs uncovered in the diagnosis process. An underlying value is technically a part of the strategy that people are following to get today's results. If this direction is actually moving people away from delivering the needed results, the underlying belief must be uprooted and removed from the system. For example, if the diagnosis reveals that many associates in the system believe *"the boss knows best,"* and this is causing cycle times to be too long, then this belief must be countered. As part of the new strategy, one might define a value or operating principle such as, *"whoever sees a problem is responsible to solve it."* The new value promotes what associates *should* have in their mind rather than the current self-defeating belief.

Once the strategy has been defined with as many (or as few) elements as desired, the organization then can set measurable short-term objectives and goals that will lead to the strategy's fulfillment.

The second half of this step is to define a few organizational capabilities that will be required to deliver the strategy. Must we have speed, accountability and strategic clarity to deliver the strategy? Or are the requirements for customer connectivity, innovation, and collaboration the critical few? The combination of the Strategy & Organizational Capabilities give you the design specs for the rest of the organizational elements.

Step Two. Design the Organizational Systems to successfully deliver the Strategy. In organization design, as in architecture, *form follows function.* Therefore, the organizational systems should be derived from the strategy/capabilities, not the other way around. This is a complicated step, one that requires more explanation than can be given here. In the coming chapters I will review some approaches and design tools that have helped many organizations dramatically improve their results. The basic sequence, however, is quite simple. Design the Processes first, and then align Structure and Rewards and finally the People systems.

Step Three. This step calls for the organization designers to take a step back from the new strategy and organizational systems they have put together and consider if the present culture has any "organizational viruses" that might defeat the chosen design. An organizational virus is a deeply-rooted underlying belief or behavior that is a barrier to the progress you seek. You may uncover such viruses during the diagnosis process. However, there may be some viruses that will specifically attack the organization design you are proposing. Many design plans that are completely logical and could have been considered best practices have flopped in implementation because they were attacked by such viruses.

For example, one client told us their culture was one in which everyone was always inventing something new. A new product would be conceptualized, initial testing and prototyping would be completed, and then everyone's attention would leap forward to find the next big idea. Someone else was supposed to finalize the product and introduce it into the market place. This virus (often a strength becomes a virus if taken to extremes) of "find the new idea" was hurting them because very few of their big ideas became commercially viable. If this virus were left untreated, what do you suppose the organization's response would be to a new system requiring the inventor to continue with the project through final market release? Some inventors might leave, in hopes of finding another inventor's paradise somewhere else. Some might quickly go through the motions to deliver the product even if it might lead to surprises in the market place and bring disappointing results.

This practical step invites you to check for some unseen forces that might defeat a well-constructed organization design and plan to eradicate them during the design implementation phase.

Step Four. Design falls short unless it is able to accomplish a lasting change in the daily behaviors so that the desired results are produced. I have been disappointed at the number of organization designs that have never truly delivered what they were capable of delivering because the implementation phase was done hastily or ignored altogether. Remember the immortal words of Peter Drucker, "Plans are only good intentions unless they immediately degenerate into hard work."

Effectively implementing an organization design is hard work that requires several things:

1. An action plan for rolling out the new design. Who needs to do what by when, with whom to transition from the current design to the better design?

2. A commitment plan that anticipates how the different stakeholders might react to the changes and also plans to earn their commitment to the new order of things. Who needs to make it happen, help it happen, let it happen or stay out of the process? A well-conceived commitment plan is one way of eradicating organizational viruses.

3. A communication plan that tells everyone affected by the new design why things will be different in the future and why. This plan needs to incorporate elements from the previous two planning steps.

4. A monitoring plan to track progress on items 1-3, defining the metrics to be used and communication methods to be employed.

5. A contingency plan that addresses any developments in implementation that do not match expectations for the new design. What happens if the new structure does not improve collaboration between functions? What if the leadership

training does not change underlying beliefs? Who should come together to decide what needs to be done? Thought should be given to such questions in the planning phase rather during the rollout phase when emotions can run high and distort the big picture.

Feel free to use any other tools you have found to be successful. Just check to make sure these five elements are included (in whatever form) as you move forward.

Step Five. This is the final sanity check for the design process: to predict what effect the new culture (after successful implementation of the design) will have on results. Will you in fact be better, faster, cheaper (or whatever your intended targets are) than competition? Will the associates actually perform at the needed levels? Is the logic between the new behaviors in culture and the desired results clear and compelling? If all answers are affirmative, then the project is ready to be launched!

Conclusion

The Organization Systems Model is a roadmap for the journey of designing your organization to stay at the top of the lifecycle. It can be used to keep the "big picture" perspective when understanding today's situation and designing for tomorrow's success. When applied with interactive group processes, it can yield significant diagnostic insights in a short period of time. It can also help you keep the ecological order of all the key elements when designing the organization to get the results you want.

PART TWO:
The Organizational Survival Code

5
Strategizing to Meet Stakeholder Needs

"Profit is like oxygen. If you don't have enough, you won't be around for long; but if you think life is about breathing, you're missing something."

—*RUSSELL ACKOFF*

"The trouble with most of us is that we would rather be ruined by praise than saved by criticism."

—*NORMAN VINCENT PEALE*

A member of a volunteer group called one night to inform his team leader he would not be able to take part in their project that evening. They were short staffed as it was and now this! The team leader called a good friend, Pete, to see if he might be able to help out.

"I'm sorry," Pete said, "but my daughter is flying in from out of town and my wife and I are going to meet her at the airport."

"Oh," said the team leader with some disappointment in his voice.

"Wait a minute," Pete said. "You're in a tough spot, aren't you?"

"Well, yes," the team leader replied.

"My wife can pick up our daughter," Pete said. "I will make it my business to be there tonight."

As soon as the team leader heard the words, "I will make it my business to be there..." he knew his problem was solved. He knew he could count on Pete.

Pete's choice of words in this example got me thinking about the many organizations I associate with in a typical month. I invite you to do the same. How many employers, food stores, banks, schools, restaurants, government agencies, insurance companies, hospitals, physicians, repair specialists, builders, airlines, retailers, professional-service firms and gas stations truly make our business their business? How many of them place as much value on our needs as we do? Yet, those few who do this earn our unwavering loyalty.

As I address the subject of aligning what your organization does with your stakeholders' needs, think of Pete's statement and remember the objective is to *make their business your business*.

The Stakeholder Ecosystem

You will recall one of the natural laws of living systems is ecological order—all elements of a natural ecosystem either fit into the order of things or they perish. Every organization exists in an ecosystem of stakeholder needs. A stakeholder is anyone who has a stake in the organization's well-being—customers, suppliers, associates, communities, families. If your organization would survive over time, you must (1) identify which important stakeholder needs you intend to address, (2) commit all your organizational resources to meet those needs (make their business your business), and (3) consistently fulfill the needs.

The key in any ecosystem, even that of stakeholder needs, is balance. To shape and maintain a healthy balance with stakeholder needs, remember three points:

- **You won't be able to meet all stakeholder needs.** Many will contradict each other. Some may be outside the scope of what your business strategy is. Trying to optimize all the pieces will suboptimize the whole—your organization! One of the critical leadership tasks is to choose which needs to fulfill and which to pass up.
- **In the long run, the best way to serve any one stakeholder is to meet all *critical* stakeholder needs.** Not every need,

but the critical few for each that will make or break your relationship. As with any ecosystem, whenever you seek to maximize the interests of one element at the expense of another, you may well end up hurting the very ones you are seeking to help. For example, what if you tried to maximize the interests of your customers in isolation and at the expense of your associates' or community's needs? The result might be associate turnover and violations of the law to the point that you were no longer able to serve your customers well. Similarly, maximizing associates' needs for job security and income in isolation of market realities might place you in such an unprofitable position that you would have to close your doors—thereby destroying the very security and income you were trying to assure.

■ Japan's Association of Corporate Executives understood this ecosystem when it published this statement: *"Traditionally, the relationship of companies to their stakeholders has been expressed using such terms as 'putting the customer first,' 'putting the employees first,' or 'maintaining stable shareholders.' We, however, believe that the term 'stakeholder' should be defined to include any party that plays a role in supporting an organization's long-term success. Thus, every manager needs to be aware that the organization's survival is dependent not only on its customers, employees, shareholders, and distributors, but in a larger sense on the global community as a whole. Working to build mutual trust with all of these stakeholders is of vital importance and is in essence the definition of management."*

■ **If you fail to satisfy critical needs for any stakeholder, you may lose their support, disrupting your delicate balance.** You might fall as they pull away. This is the frustrating, but real, paradox of an ecosystem. The best way to care for any one part of the system is to care for all parts. But, in the attempt to serve all, you can't afford to shortchange any one's few, critical needs.

Now comes the most challenging part of the whole equation: *these stakeholder needs are ever changing.* You can't just determine today's needs and organize yourself to meet them and then sit back. You have to develop a system to regularly take the pulse of all these stakeholders over time. What you need is a dynamic information system.

In the following sections, I will share some tools and approaches that I have seen successfully align corporations with their stakeholders.

Stakeholder Feedback

Stakeholder feedback helps you monitor the strength of your relationship with all those whose support is essential for you to fulfill your strategy. Here are some major elements that make stakeholder feedback useful:

■ It measures how well you are meeting the critical needs for each major stakeholder.

- It's not a one-time event, but a process that is repeated periodically.
- It's used as part of a larger process to reaffirm or redefine your business strategy.
- It provides information for both the diagnosis and design specifications to improve what you do.

Notice that in these four bullets I have said nothing about surveys, questionnaires, or performance appraisal instruments! Some or all of these may have a part to play in gathering stakeholder feedback, but the end state is more than its components. The right process or system for gathering stakeholder feedback is something you will need to design for your specific situation and set of stakeholders.

Some years ago, Jan Carlzon, then CEO of Scandinavian Air Lines (SAS), coined the phrase "the moments of truth" to describe how well an organization fulfills its stakeholder needs. These moments determine whether or not customers or other stakeholders stay with you. He estimated SAS's annual business was made up of 50 million such moments, each lasting an average of 15 seconds. For SAS customers, they include such things as:

- You get the seat you reserved.
- The magazines you like to read are available on board.
- You are served the special meal you ordered.
- The flight attendants are competent and cheerful.

- You take off and arrive on time.
- Your baggage arrives promptly and in good condition.
- Any problems are solved quickly and courteously.

These moments of truth define *what the customer wants to see.* This is a healthy point of departure for fitting into the order of your stakeholders' needs. *What are the moments of truth as seen by your organization's key stakeholders?*

One good way to identify these moments of truth is to ask your shareholders, customers, suppliers, employees, and community agencies what they hope to gain from their relationship with you. You may be surprised by what you learn, as Fred was in the following example:

Fred was a vice president of a Fortune 500 company. As part of a major restructuring effort in his company, he was asked to interview some retailers who sold his products. His assignment was to understand their moments of truth when dealing with his company. After the interviews, Fred made a most interesting statement, "I've been with this company 27 years, but had never actually spoken to a retail customer until last week. I was amazed at some of the things they want us to do for them. Many of the things that were important to them were administrative or service items. I had no idea they wanted these things from us. The wonderful part is that if we can deliver these things, they will help our customers, they will help our business, and it won't cost us a penny. We can do these things right away and strengthen our business."

Whether stakeholder feedback contains surprises or confirmation of what you already know, it is one of the keys to surviving through changing times.

Strategy Check

All stakeholder feedback is important to help you see the big picture. But how do you know what to act on and what to leave as is? The answer to this question can only be found by consulting your organization's strategy. For instance, if your strategy is to be the low cost producer, customer feedback that says you aren't as good as the "high price brand" will probably not set off any alarms or call for any response on your part. However, feedback that says customers don't care about the price anymore should be studied very carefully. If this development is more than just a short-term trend, sticking to your low-cost producer strategy probably will move you down the lifecycle and out of business. You may need to adjust your strategy or make other changes in response to the new reality.

Look at your stakeholder feedback through the lens of your business strategy and ask yourself questions like these:

■ What are most critical needs of each stakeholder group? What are the "must haves" from their perspective for continuing to do business with us?

■ How well are we meeting these critical needs at the present time?

■ From the stakeholders' perspective, what things do we do really well?

■ What are the few things the stakeholders would like to see us change immediately?

■ What external changes do we foresee that will require us to do some things differently in order to continue to meet our stakeholders' most critical needs? How must we respond to these changes?

■ Which stakeholder needs are "off strategy" from our perspective? (That is, they want us to do "X," but that is not aligned with our strategy.) Can we truly afford to say "no" to these needs?

■ Are there any new stakeholders or new critical needs from existing stakeholders that define new business opportunities for us?

■ Bottom line–what changes (if any) should we make to our strategy? What changes should we make to how we are implementing our strategy?

"When you're up to your neck in alligators, it's hard to remember that you originally came in to drain the swamp." This popular saying is all too true in our organizational world. Take the time to gather stakeholder feedback at regular intervals and evaluate the data from a strategic framework and you will be able to handle the alligators AND drain the swamp.

Benchmarking

Part of the task of "fitting into the order of things" is to understand how well others (your peers and competitors) are fitting into the order of things. One way to get in touch with this is by benchmarking what you do versus others. Benchmarking has become popular in the age of downsizing, but there is no natural law that says benchmarking must result in downsizing. The appropriate action step must be defined by the context of the business environment and by alignment with the organization's strategy. Many organizations benchmark their work processes, staffing levels, and financial measures against the best in their industry simply to understand where they stand in the global marketplace. This feedback helps them choose realistic, but challenging improvement targets.

The most dramatic breakthroughs have come, however, from those organizations that use a true global benchmark: not just the best in one industry, but the very best in the world at whatever is being studied. Here's an example of what I mean:

One manufacturing company had been struggling for years to increase the speed of its production changeovers. Typically the production team needed 72 hours to readjust the equipment settings to run a different product. But customer demand for product variations was driving the need for faster turnaround times and the company was beginning to lose business because of its slow changeovers. Finally a team member, who was also a NASCAR driver, got the idea of treating the changeover process like a pit stop. "How would we handle this changeover if we were a pit crew?" he asked his team. With this new mindset, they made process changes that accomplished the same complicated adjustments in a mere three hours!

As this manufacturer learned, the best in the world at changeovers was not one of its peers. Another example:

A produce wholesaler approached me one day after reading that P&G and Walmart hoped to reduce their inventory levels (amount of product stored in their warehouses) from 21 days to nine days through their new partnership. "I couldn't help but smile when I read that in the Wall Street Journal," the produce man said. "If I had even nine days of inventory in my warehouses, I'd have a lot of spoiled fruit and vegetables to throw away. I'll bet if you at P&G treated Crest toothpaste as if it were perishable, you'd find a way to cut those nine days down to two."

What a way to jolt your assumptions! Just apply this global notion of benchmarking against some of your most critical processes:

- Who is the best in the world at transmitting information simultaneously to many geographically-dispersed locations?
- Who is the best teaching organization in the world?
- Who manufactures something with zero defects, with the lowest case costs, and with unparalleled flexibility?
- Who is the best at serving their customers?
- Who has the fastest cycle time from product idea to product on the shelf?
- Who makes sound decisions quickly, yet with real input and buy-in from many parties?

Do some serious benchmarking in the areas of strategic leverage for your organization and you will find new opportunities to handle challenges and opportunities in your competitive arena.

Aligning All Associates With Stakeholder Values

One of the most difficult tasks facing any organization is to get alignment between what associates focus on every day and the critical stakeholder values. Alignment of these two produces survival. Misalignment drives you down the lifecycle. Many organizations have used a balanced scorecard, a short list of key success targets representing all critical stakeholder needs, to get this alignment.

US Synthetic (USS), a manufacturer of the Polycrystalline Diamond Cutter (PDC) used for drilling in oil exploration, has gone a measure beyond the traditional balanced scorecard. USS' "Strategy Tree," a framework that captures the company's strategic intent, is not constructed and monitored by senior management alone. It is a living monitor of the company's vital signs and specific versions of it are crafted by all work units and their team members to help them keep their commitments to their many stakeholders. As you can see, USS views itself as much more than just a transactional provider of PDC cutters; it aims to improve the lives of its primary stakeholders:

Why is the Strategy Tree a measure beyond the balanced scorecard? Here are a few features:

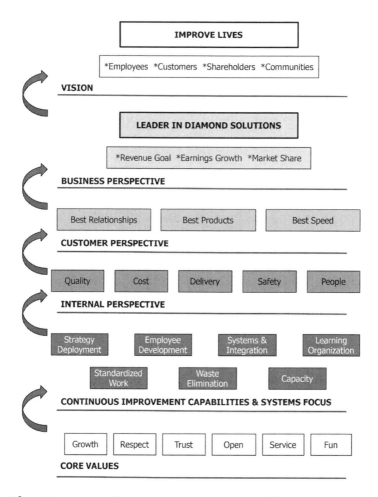

- The Strategy Tree gives very specific attention to the needs of all major stakeholders: employees, customers, shareholders and communities. All other items on the tree are specific needs of these stakeholders.

- The measures and targets specified are taken from stakeholder feedback and benchmarking studies in USS' industry.

- The major categories and targets on the tree are modified periodically to ensure they match what stakeholders need *today*.

- People at USS actually take the Strategy Tree seriously! A large Strategy Tree poster is prominently positioned in the production center and corporate results are updated frequently during each shift. Just as important, however, is the updating that all work units and associates do every few minutes to their specific Strategy Tree measures. The team reports its results and any operating issues at least every two hours to the team leader. Feedback occurs spontaneously on the production floor and contributes to updating the scoreboard. Associates follow up on the most persistent problems, using continuous improvement tools to identify problem root causes and eliminate them. Thus, the USS Strategy Tree enables the real experts who make PDCs to solve problems and deliver value to all stakeholders.

US Synthetic today is reaping a bounteous harvest from seeds planted 30 years ago by its founder Louis Pope. Use of the Strategy Tree is one reason why the company has grown to be the market leader (capturing more than 30 percent of the global market for PDC cutters).

I highly recommend these tools: stakeholder feedback, strategy check, benchmarking and whatever application you choose of the Strategy Tree described here. Apply them to your particular situation as seems sensible. Smaller units may not need a lengthy document. Your "Strategy Tree" may consist of a few clear priorities that address your stakeholders' most critical needs. Or, you may need precise instruments in each category for a large, global organization. The aim, remember, is to have all associates on the same page when *making the stakeholders' business your business.*

A Case in Point

Will this really make a difference? Here is the case of one leader who managed to bring order out of chaos.

A study of a European organization's effectiveness involved interviewing key leaders in nine different countries. One of the themes that emerged from the interviews was how confused people were about the strategic direction. These leaders said they received one set of priorities from their general manager, another set of priorities from their functional boss and other (often conflicting) priorities from their direct supervisor, customers or Headquarters.

The only exception to this state of confusion was in Mary's subsidiary. Mary was the general manager who studied her local market and derived from her research what the organization needed to deliver. She summarized her analysis into three priorities:

- Double the volume
- Triple the profits
- Run a "seamless" operation (no internal misalignments)

When leaders in Mary's organization were interviewed, every one of them listed these three priorities as "their" priorities for the business. In contrast to peers in all the other countries, no one complained about an unclear strategic direction. Coincidentally, Mary's organization was further along in achieving its objectives than anyone else.

Whether your situation can be covered by three strategic priorities or requires a more comprehensive balanced scorecard, you will see the difference if you can help everyone commit to the few things they can do to deliver what their stakeholders need.

Subordinate Everything Else to Strategy

I dare not leave this subject without acknowledging a very human and very real dynamic that comes with any feedback exercise. You might be surprised, shocked, disappointed, and upset to learn what different stakeholders really think about your organization. If you allow your pride, ego, or your assumption of reality to govern your response, then in that moment you rewrite your strategy. You are no longer about meeting stakeholder needs, but only your needs. All you've invested in the feedback system will now be at the mercy of your emotions or ego when it comes time to take action. Here's an example of this dynamic:

> An executive of a large drugstore company was invited to address the general managers of a Fortune 500 company. The theme of the session was "Satisfying Customer Needs." The guest speaker had prior experience as an executive with one of his audience's competitors, so he had lived on both sides of the fence. At the outset of his presentation, this executive said, "I'd like to share with you how we look at your operation; how we tend to judge your company—and all of our suppliers—from our viewpoint."

> Then he listed the following factors:
> 1. Are your products available at the time we need them?
> 2. Are your special promotions aligned with ours? (Do your "50¢ Off" coupons come at a time when we are prepared to give you maximum display space?)
> 3. What's the cycle time?
> 4. How flexible are your sales incentives? (Are they relevant to us?)
> 5. How compatible are your displays with our store arrangements?

Then he asked the audience, "How many of you have ever thought about these things?" From his own experience as a manufacturer, he knew the answer: Those in the room paid little, if any, attention to these five issues. Continuing, he then said, "We took the liberty of giving you a rating, either average, above average, or below average. And here is the report card we would fill out for you:

Desired Service	–	Average	+
1. Product available on time	☐	☑	☐
2. Alignment of promotions	☑	☐	☐
3. Cycle time	☐	☑	☐
4. Incentive flexibility	☑	☐	☐
5. Compatible displays	☑	☐	☐

It was obvious to everyone there that this evaluation was a benchmark against other companies, some of whom had to be above average. Those in the audience, naturally, had great pride in their company. They felt they were the best. What do you think happened when this customer told them they were average to below average in all five categories? People were suffering—silently—throughout the room.

Then the speaker said, "I told my associates when we did this rating, 'I can't go to this company and evaluate them like this without some kind of documentation or examples.'" So he pulled out an issue from the field for each one. Somebody wrote in and said, "They announced a special promotion on a product. We advertised it in our flyers that go out to all the houses and the color supplements in the newspapers. We advertised it for the week of February 14 and we didn't get the product until February 28." Then the speaker gave further examples, item by item, which had led to these ratings.

How do you suppose these leaders responded to this message? Of all the presenters in this three-day conference, this speaker received the lowest rating of all, and the participants' comments were very revealing: "Made sweeping generalizations from a few isolated incidents. Very opinionated with sketchy data. Hard to follow. Not logical."

What meaningful corrective action would you expect to come out of such a session? Very little, if any, as long as pride and their own belief of their performance took priority over strategy. The executives' reaction to their customer's feedback reminded me of this passage from John Steinbeck's *East of Eden:*

"I don't want advice."

"Nobody does. It's a giver's present."

But ignoring such feedback only delays—never eliminates—the results that will flow naturally from the real world. Let your primary allegiance be to your strategy rather than ego and your own comfort zone. Strategies aligned with natural laws will never lead you down the lifecycle; they can only move you up. Our own idiosyncrasies and emotions are what cause our downfall.

Conclusion

The first big step in the journey to survival is to "make your stakeholders' business your business." The place to start is by working hard to truly understand stakeholder feedback. Next comes a comparing of this feedback with your strategic intent. Does the feedback indicate your strategy should change? That you must change some operational functions to achieve your desired results? That new opportunities (or threats) are on the horizon?

Then comes the step of imagining your future potential. Just how much can you achieve? What is truly possible? What would your needed improvements look like? This is where benchmarking can serve you well.

Finally, how do you summarize your current strategic position? What do you want everyone thinking about as they go about their work? What is your "Strategy Tree" to keep you pointed on the very things that will keep you in alignment with order of things?

The answers to all these questions will become the playbook for increased organizational effectiveness and stronger business results. Revise the playbook in a timely manner and you need never fall down the lifecycle!

6
Developing a Compelling Purpose

"A system is a network of interdependent components that work together to accomplish the aim of the system. The system must have an aim. The aim must be clear to everyone in the system."

—*W. EDWARDS DEMING*

"If a man does not know what port he is steering for, no wind is favorable to him."

—*SENECA*

"It is immoral to ask people to work without purpose."

—*HORST SCHULZE*

Many organizations have taken to writing mission statements in recent years. Almost everywhere you go you see impressively framed statements hanging in corporate lobbies and conference rooms. They are referred to in annual reports and at shareholders meetings. Executives quote from them at management gatherings, but how many of these carefully crafted statements really influence what goes on every day? The following experience made me wonder about this.

I had been on the road all day, it was getting late, and I was starving! Entering a restaurant's lobby, my eyes were drawn to the mission statement on the wall behind the cash register. The statement read something like this:

> *"Our mission is*
> *to provide our customers*
> *with a high quality dining experience in a*
> *home-like atmosphere."*

This sounded awfully good to me! I was prepared to let the restaurant fulfill its mission. My eyes then moved down from the mission statement. Sitting below it and behind the cash register was an associate reading a paperback novel. She seemed totally immersed in her reading. After several seconds of standing around, I coughed gently to catch the cashier's attention.

"Oh, do you want to eat?" she asked as she looked up from her reading.

"Yes, that's why I came in."

"Over there." She pointed to a doorway as her nose again disappeared into the book.

Moving to the doorway, I saw a sea of activity with people running back and forth. I stood there waiting for a while before trying to get someone's attention. "Excuse me, could I get a table?" I asked.

"Just a minute, I'm busy," a waitress said as she scurried off to the kitchen. Eventually a woman came and seated me. There was no menu. After several minutes I got a waitress' attention, "Pardon me, could I get a menu?"

"Just a second, I'm busy." At this point I began to get the notion of what the restaurant meant by a "home-like atmosphere." In my own home this was the line my children used when asked to help get dinner ready—"Hold on! I'm busy." Slowly, I was beginning to comprehend the restaurant's mission statement!

The food was late, cold, not very tasty, and I had to compete with the novel for the cashier's attention in order to pay my bill. I walked out of the restaurant vowing never to go in again. Yet the mission statement had been so promising. My conclusion was no one really took it seriously.

Interestingly enough, I was in another city some time later and passed by another one of these restaurants. All the windows were boarded up. Today this company is out of business.

Could there be a connection between owners, managers, and associates not taking their own mission statement seriously and the company's failure to survive? If they really developed a high quality dining experience and home-like atmosphere, would they go out of business?

Research tells us this restaurant's mission statement experience is typical of most organizations. Some years ago, a survey found that 85 percent of the Fortune 500 companies had a corporate mission statement, but only 15 percent of those who had them used them when making critical, daily business decisions. In other words, only 64 of the largest 500 companies were getting any value from having a mission statement. Small wonder so many people around the world are cynical when the topic of mission statements is raised. More disturbing than cynicism, however, is the misalignment between these organizations and natural laws. Some companies issue a new version of the mission and cloak it under the title of "Purpose" or "Vision" to convey that it is "different" than the previous mission.

The key point here is that any living system that does not have a compelling purpose (by whatever name) is at the mercy of the environment's driving forces.

In this chapter, I will review some principles and processes that can spell the difference between a compelling and meaningless purpose. My focus will be on the dynamics that are required to shape a common direction out of the many self-interests you and your stakeholders have.

What Makes a Purpose Compelling?

What is it about a compelling purpose that harnesses people's energies? What is it that, if missing, turns a purpose statement into just one more mundane administrative process? Earl Nightingale identified a natural law of human behavior that he called the strangest secret in the world: *We become what we think about.* Let's test this premise.

What did the members of the restaurant staff think about? We know what was on the wall, *but what was in their mind*? If we could read their thoughts, they might look something like this:

Our Mission is to:

- Put in the time required to do the job.
- Do as we're told.
- Depend on the customer's good will.
- Go with the flow.
- Minimize our inconvenience.
- Endure until quitting time.

This statement is certainly closer to what the restaurant associates thought about than the words on the wall and the restaurant became what its people thought about—reactive, harried, and mediocre. Isn't it ironic that as their life became easier (e.g., fewer customers), the company went out of business?

We become what we think about. Sometimes people don't think about anything. Their actions are habitual, or emotional, or expedient in the moment. They react to each moment and the organization, in turn, reacts momentarily to things. If this is the situation in your organization, you will never be able to "make their business your business." The dynamics of a compelling purpose are:

- Focused on the highest priority stakeholder moments of truth.
- Chosen and prioritized by all members through an interactive process.
- Translated by each person into personal responsibilities and actions.
- To hold everyone accountable to deliver on priorities and to subordinate everything else.

Here is an example from U.S. history that illustrates these points. Inscribed today on the First Parish Unitarian—Universalist Church on the Lexington Common in Lexington, Massachusetts—is a pledge adopted in that township's second meeting house in 1773. It reads: "…we shall be ready to sacrifice our estates and everything dear in life, yea, and life itself in support of the common cause."

As you may know, on April 19, 1775, Lexington was the scene of the first battle of the Revolutionary War. The "shot heard 'round the world" was not fired in a moment of hot-tempered lawlessness; it was the natural consequence of the British army coming face to face with those who had been mobilized by the Lexington pledge. These words were very compelling!

The Lexington pledge contains two important ingredients: (1) "a common cause" and (2) the commitment to sacrifice everything else for it. In our individualistic world, it is hard for us to remember the things we have in common when our culture emphasizes self-interest.

Today's organizations draft purpose statements in the hope that, like Lexington's, they will mobilize people to do the right thing in any situation. Unfortunately, we have seen how most of their efforts turn out. If your organization has such a statement, look at it now. Does it compel you to action? Are you mobilized to sacrifice other dear things for the common cause?

Now, *suppose you took your purpose seriously?* What steps would you need to take as a leader to reach each person's heart and mind? Those who have followed this principle have given attention to three areas: (1) Content, (2) Process and (3) Practice.

Content: Tapping Into Stakeholders' Moments of Truth

Read enough purpose statements and after awhile you will see they all look very similar. There is an important reason for this: *most people and organizations have the same fundamental desires and needs.* An effective purpose captures these and commits the organization to fulfill them. People (and organizations) have five basic needs:

- **Physical**— the need to survive.
- **Social**— the need to be part of a primary group.
- **Emotional**— the need for acceptance, hope, security
- **Mental**— the need to learn new things
- **Spiritual**— the need to be consistent with one's personal values

Professors John A. Pearce II and Fred David published a research study[3] that affirmed the need for addressing all five needs. Pearce and David wrote to the Fortune 500 companies and asked for a copy of their mission statement. From the 61 mission statements they obtained to study, a content analysis revealed eight topics were generally covered. In other words, every point in the mission statements could be categorized under one of these eight headings:

1. Specifying target customers and markets *(Physical & Social)*
2. Commitment to principal products or services *(Physical)*
3. Identifying the intended geographic domain *(Physical)*

3   Pearce, John A II and Fred David, Corporate mission statements: The bottom line, *Academy of Management Executive, 1987, Vol. 1, No. 2, pp. 109-116.*

4. Describing the core technologies *(Physical & Mental)*

5. Sharing plans for survival, growth, profitability *(Physical)*

6. Disclosing basic beliefs, values, philosophy *(Spiritual)*

7. Expressing the company's view of itself *(Spiritual & Emotional)*

8. Stating the firm's desired public image *(Spiritual)*

Next, they broke down the performance of these 61 companies into four quadrants by profitability. Though the eight elements were found in many of the statements, Pearce and David identified three that were present in the top 25 percent and were absent in the other 75 percent. Which of these eight do you think correlate with high performance?

If you guessed #6, #7, and #8, you are right! Those organizations whose missions focused everyone's attention on the full list (and all five basic needs) outperformed those who neglected some spiritual and emotional needs.

Thus we see that one key ingredient for a purpose statement is to connect with all five of these basic needs.

Process: Involvement Brings Commitment

Many leaders frequently are shocked and disappointed by others' reactions to their carefully written purpose statement. I have seen it all too often—senior managers proudly unveil the statement only to hear comments like:

- "It sounds like motherhood and apple pie."
- "Sounds like every other statement I've seen recently."
- "It took you how long to write this little statement?"

Such expressions are your first clue that these people are not yet called to action! The process you use will greatly affect the degree of commitment, cynicism, or apathy that may exist toward your purpose. If a few leaders come back from an executive retreat and present a new purpose statement to the organization, the chances are very slim that people will find the statement compelling. In contrast, the following steps have earned enthusiastic followers in a number of companies:

- **Process initiated by senior management:** One sure way to kill commitment is to develop the statement without senior management's deep conviction. Some organizations have used a grass-roots approach in an attempt to get widespread commitment. Such approaches tend to be "politically correct," but may not capture the hearts and minds of the senior managers. I recommend *beginning* the process at the top to ensure the leadership, commitment, and involvement of senior managers. If the purpose is to come alive, it must be compelling to them too.

- **Significant, intense, early involvement of others:** the risk of beginning the purpose shaping process at the top is that it may stop there. Remember the natural law, "We become what we think about." We *all* become what we think about—*every one of us.* Once you understand this, how could you even think of writing a statement only at the top or only at the grass roots? Begin at the top, but make sure you get significant, intense, early involvement of others so that they own it. Involvement doesn't mean hearing about it in a mass meeting. Involvement means contributing to it, shaping it, deeply understanding its impact on yourself and others.

- **Stakeholder review and feedback:** one way of getting involvement is to open up the process for genuine review and feedback from all stakeholders. This process can get the purpose's key elements into all the hearts and minds of those who must work together to bring it to life.

- **Integrated sub-unit statements:** if you really want people to take the purpose seriously, have them translate the corporate statement into a statement for their department or work team. Doing this accomplishes two things: (1) it ensures individuals have understood the company purpose, and (2) it applies the corporate statement to their own specific responsibilities.

Practice: The Purpose as a Constitution

With the content igniting the flame and a process designed to create something compelling for all members, the purpose should be positioned to have great impact on the organization. What else do you need? It's important to remember that the purpose is only a statement of good intentions. It can only make a difference when it is put to use in daily practice.

Those who take their statement seriously treat it like a constitution or other governmental code of law. In many nations a constitution is the supreme law of the land. Everything else is subordinated to the supreme law. If any other law, practice, system, or habit is found to be in contradiction with the constitution, it is the practice or system that must change.

This constitutional metaphor illustrates how seriously to take your purpose statement. Use the statement as the standard to evaluate everything else that goes on. Here are some practical ways to do this:

- **Introduce new associates to it** by sharing what it does and doesn't mean on a daily basis. Some organizations even use the statement to shape hiring criteria and gauge potential associates' commitment to it in the interview process.

- **Make it constantly visible to all stakeholders.** The purpose statement is prominently displayed in halls, lobbies, conference rooms, and eating/break areas. Furthermore, it is actively referenced in contracts, agreements, and other forms of written communication with suppliers, contractors, customers, and other stakeholders. Most importantly, it is consulted frequently in daily conversation, especially when decisions need to be made.

■ **Align all other organizational elements with the Purpose.** Shaping systems, structures, and habits to be aligned with the statement brings about the rare phenomenon of organizational integrity: what the organization says (purpose) and what it does (through systems, structure, and culture) are fully congruent.

■ **Review it periodically** over the long term, revising as appropriate to reflect changing conditions. In other words, treat it like a living document, not something that's written once and set in stone never to change.

Let's examine an organizational case study that illustrates how content, process and practice can come together to create a compelling purpose.

The Heartland Plant: United We Stand

For many years the "Heartland" Plant was a leading manufacturing facility for "Gillespie Enterprises", a Fortune 500 company located in the Midwest USA. Results in every measurable area were always near the top of the standings. Plant leaders always gave credit to the "outstanding people" in the plant who had set the standards and achieved impressive results. But the plant leadership team, constantly prodded by its plant manager, was always looking for ways to improve Heartland's performance.

As part of a reassessment process in 2009, a diagonal slice of the plant work force made a diagnosis of the present state. They identified some dynamics that were disturbing:

- Despite the good production numbers, teams all too often had to call in a few "heroes" to fix certain equipment problems that had shut them down. No one else on the team could solve these problems. Results came too frequently from these heroic actions, not from reliable work processes.

- Teams were focused almost exclusively on getting the immediate, short-term results, not getting to root causes and eliminating oft-occurring problems.

- With the company pushing a new reliability program, expectations were high that Heartland would lead the way in significant reliability improvements.

- The plant would not be able to achieve reliability leadership numbers if the status quo prevailed.

- Another symptom of the focus on immediate, short-term results was the reality that the plant did not focus enough on what the overall business needed from it in terms of leadership, people development, process improvements and innovation.

The group of 28 plant members who identified these issues then had to wrestle with the task of developing a clear and compelling purpose. The plant purpose statement aimed to achieve two things: (1) identify the few things the plant wanted to be known for by its key stakeholders and (2) excite Heartland associates enough so that they would think about the purpose constantly—and bring it to life as they worked.

The issues the Heartland Plant wanted to be clear about in their purpose statement included:

- How do we honor our successful past and yet get everyone to see the bigger picture?
- How do we eliminate our dependency on the "heroes" without offending them?

Here is the statement they came up with:

We are Trusted Partners because we have:
- **Extraordinary People**
- **Continuously-Improving Processes**
- **Breakthrough Performance**

This statement proved to be an effective focal point that every associate in the plant could understand and rally behind. Notice how these very few words connect with all five basic needs:

- **Physical:** breakthrough performance
- **Social:** extraordinary people; trusted partners
- **Emotional:** *trusted* partners

■ **Mental:** continuously-improving processes

■ **Spiritual:** the entire statement reaffirmed core plant values that everyone truly wanted to experience in Heartland

Purpose Statements: Product or Process?

As we conclude this chapter, it should be evident that there is more to a purpose statement than the piece of paper (the product). It is my strong belief that the magic of such statements is to be found in the processes used to create and nurture them. *The process is indeed the product.*

Once you understand that a purpose's process is the product, you won't make the common mistake of saying it is "done" when the piece of paper has been produced. If you have used quality stakeholder feedback to help shape it and it truly represents some universal values, then the content won't change very often. Any changes that are made will come slowly and only after a thorough review. Like a constitution, your statement will be a changeless core amidst all the other changes that surround you.

But your work isn't "done" just because the statement is hanging on the wall. You must keep the process alive for those who join the organization later, for those who may forget the direction in moments of crisis, and for those who don't seek its guidance when new situations arise.

Never forget a purpose statement's process is the product. You may read others' statements and come away unimpressed, or fail to see the difference between them and dozens of similar statements. With such statements, beauty is in the eye of the beholder. It's not important whether or not *you* are moved by the Heartland Plant's purpose statement. What is important is that *Heartland associates* are compelled to action—swift, aligned, consistent, targeted action that brings great results to align with increasingly higher performance expectations.

7
Designing Work Processes that Deliver High Quality

"As you ramble on through life,
Whatever be your goal,
Keep your eye upon the doughnut
And not upon the hole!"

— AUTHOR UNKNOWN

"Plans are only good intentions unless
they immediately degenerate into hard work."

— PETER DRUCKER

Even a compelling purpose statement is, at face value, only a statement of good intentions. These good intentions must be turned into concrete work and, as the German proverb reminds us, "the devil is in the details." Defining the core processes of the organization are first essential details to be spelled out after developing a compelling purpose.

Despite years of giving attention to Quality methodologies and incentives, too many managers still focus excessively on the hole (their specific set of tasks) and not the doughnut (the process stream that actually delivers results). In this chapter, I will review some principles and approaches that can help your organization balance attention to specific tasks and their processes so that organizationally, you walk your talk.

Ritz-Carlton Hotels: Deriving Processes from Purpose

In 1983, entrepreneur William Johnson of Atlanta lured away Horst Schulze from Hyatt Hotels to start up a new company, The Ritz-Carlton Hotel Company. Although analysts said the hotel industry was overpopulated and would not see any new successful entries, William and Horst were convinced they could compete with the best in the business.

And compete they have indeed! From a single hotel in Boston in 1983, Ritz-Carlton has grown to be an industry leader with some 90 hotels in 25 countries. It is well above the industry average in occupancy rates. Its employee turnover is about one third of its competitors. Its financial performance is more than satisfactory to the entrepreneurs who own each of the hotel properties. (Yes, that's right. The Ritz-Carlton Hotel Company owns no property; it is the managing entity for each property's owners.) Twice it has won the coveted Baldrige Quality Award in the service category. Its overall customer engagement score now ranks above the 90th percentile as measured by the Gallup organization.

Almost invisible behind the smiling, friendly, service-passionate hotel staff is a remarkable case study in organizational alignment and adherence to the organizational survival code.

THE RITZ-CARLTON®

The Ritz-Carlton is a place where the genuine care and comfort of our guests is our highest mission. We pledge to provide the finest personal service and facilities for our guests who will always enjoy a warm, relaxed yet refined ambience.

The Ritz-Carlton experience enlivens the senses, instills well-being, and fulfills even the unexpressed wishes and needs of our guests.

The centerpiece that drives everything good that Ritz-Carlton does is its credo.

As impressive as these words are to the would-be guest, Ritz-Carlton's success has come from the way it has operationalized the credo's good intentions into everyday guest experiences all over the world.

To launch its successful formula, Ritz-Carlton's founders broke down the credo into 18 core work processes, each aimed at delivering what the guests expect and need from their hotel stay. Let's go through the steps of deriving core work processes from a credo.

Look at the credo and pull out its key elements. Using the credo's own verbiage, these elements are:

- guest care
- guest comfort
- personal service
- finest facilities
- warm, relaxed, refined ambience
- enliven senses
- instill well-being
- fulfill even unexpressed wishes and needs

Ritz-Carlton executives asked themselves, "What do we need to do for each guest to deliver on these promises to them?" and they answered this question from the viewpoint of the guest. This led to the identification of 18 core processes such as reservations, valet parking, reception, concierge, housekeeping, guest room preventive maintenance, sales, purchasing, laundry valet, room service, business center, restaurants, etc. Then, the executives defined the steps in each of these processes that would deliver care, comfort, ambience, and enable them to fulfill even unexpressed needs. Through the years, each of these processes is continuously improved by carefully researched recommendations from associates at each hotel.

Note that the 18 core processes are *process* titles, not departmental titles. This is intentional. It enables the hotel associates to consider first *what* should be done before assigning *who* should do it. The room service process cuts across many department lines: restaurant, bell captain and purchasing among others. Structural integrity comes from aligning all required organizational resources in each core process, not from setting new objectives for existing departments.

Getting the process right may be very disruptive to the current division of labor. "Fulfilling even the unexpressed wishes and needs of our guests" at the reception desk requires alignment from several departments within the hotel. It is healthy to temporarily ignore current departmental structures and focus instead on what has to happen task-wise to bring the core process to life. As you will see, the division of labor will be considered once the ideal process has been outlined.

Design Processes to Deliver Quality

Quality Management (QM) is one of those organizational tools that unfortunately has become a fad in many corporations. Facing the oil crisis and the emergence of Japan as a major global competitor in the 1970s, many companies turned to QM to stay in the competitive race. An enormous amount of time and money was spent on QM—training associates, developing statistical process controls, qualifying internal resources to serve as consultants and specific project work to eliminate waste and rework and increase efficiency and control. Consultants such as W. Edwards Deming, Joseph M. Juran, and Phillip Crosby became gurus who helped corporate leaders catch the vision of producing high quality products and services.

Some companies erroneously believe they are "finished" with QM and have moved on to other things. I observed this first hand when I was making a presentation at a major corporation a few years ago. This client had invested heavily in all of the above categories. When I mentioned the name of Deming to the large HR audience, a client whispered to me, "These people haven't heard of Deming." I was stunned. Deming used to be a household word in this company. Hundreds of associates were engaged in following the Quality guru's advice. Much good was accomplished during this time. What happened to QM? Was it just a flavor of the month?

Apparently so in this company. Note that Quality Process Design is linked with Survival Code principle #3: *"Develop processes and systems to consistently deliver high quality outputs."* Today there are new initiatives in the world based on the same QM principles of yesteryear: Six Sigma and Lean Manufacturing to name just two. Regardless of what you call it or which methodologies you use, the aim of the QM tool is based on principles that stand the test of time.

Quality Process Design requires (1) defining the core processes that are derived from the strategy; (2) mapping out the specific steps of each core process; (3) ensuring a free-flowing execution of each step by eliminating artificial barriers, redundancy, rework, or delays; and (4) constantly partnering with the customers and suppliers in the process to innovate and continuously improve the process as stakeholders require. Laying out the process steps is not terribly difficult. Getting the process to be free flowing is another matter.

Getting Rid of Bureaucracy

Usually one has to "de-bureaucratize" a process to make it free flowing. Bureaucracy has come to be synonymous with ineffectiveness and customer alienation. It is actually a philosophy of organization. I will explore it in detail in the next chapter. We will give our attention here to only one of bureaucracy's tenets: to break down work to its smallest possible cycle or step. This breaks up a process and, if different people are responsible for each step, introduces organizational complexity into the process. Let's examine this dynamic with a simple example.

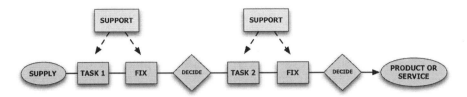

This diagram shows a very basic process initiated by a **supply** of information or material and culminating in a **product or service** delivered to a customer. The throughput consists of **Task 1** (doing something to transform the supplied resource into something more suited to the customer's needs), **Fix** (repairing or correcting any errors made in Task 1), **Support** (giving help, information, expertise, etc.), **Decide** (quality inspection or approval to move on) and **Task 2** (doing something additional to transform the information or material into a product or service that the customer desires) with its **Fix, Support** and **Decide** functions.

Some operations have separate departments for each of the functions listed above. The supplier is from one unit, the Task 1 person is in another unit, Fix in still another unit and so forth. What are the implications of this structure on the process?

What are the implications to your work if someone outside your work group or unit has to provide the next critical action or resource? There is usually a delay, some duplication of effort or possibly rework. These artificial barriers to the process arise from organizational choices. When people get involved in only one step of a process; they tend to focus on the hole (their piece), not the doughnut (the entire process). Individual actions may become misaligned with organizational strategies and require additional work to correct.

Many years ago, social scientists at England's Tavistock Institute of Human Relations experimented with different models of organizational boundaries. Through the decades that have followed, Tavistock's principles for boundary design have consistently provided a valuable enhancement to the bureaucratic model. These design principles are:

1. **Align all organizational boundaries with a change of state, or a tangible output, of the material or information being processed.** For example, raw materials are transformed through various stages into a finished product. Information is updated, expanded, and synthesized to yield more value to customers. The tangible outputs of the various stages of the work process are noticeable because they represent a *change in the physical state* of what is being processed. Updating, expanding and synthesizing raw data all change the state of that information (raw data → report). There is a tangible output associated with each state change. In our process example, there are only two tangible outputs: (1) when Task 1 transforms the supplied resource into a product form and (2) when Task 2 converts it into the final product. The other steps give support (or fix/restore the desired state of Tasks 1 and 2), but don't provide any additional tangible output other than what should have come out of the original task.

2. **Organize work units and teams around these natural boundaries UNLESS:**

   ■ **Technology is so complex that the steps must be divided up.** If the process above were for producing a two-piece, simple toy, then one individual or group could do it all. If the process were for assembling different systems for a space shuttle, the steps would need to be divided up.

   ■ **The territory required to complete the process is so large that one group could not do it effectively.** Manufacturing the two-piece toy could be done in one room. Manufacturing all systems for the space shuttle would have to be done simultaneously at different sites. Expecting one team to do all of these steps would be unrealistic.

   ■ **The Time horizon for different steps is so different that putting them together would be self-defeating.** If the process required 24-hour, seven-day coverage, then one person or team would be overwhelmed. Or, if Task 1 was scientific research and Task 2 was testing a product prototype, then it is doubtful that one person/group could do both very well because of the long-range/short-range differences. Good research requires years of study and invention; testing a prototype requires a here-and-now project mindset.

Based solely on tangible outputs, there are only three justifiable units in this process example: Supply, Task 1 (including all fixes, support, and decision making) and Task 2 (including all fixes, support, and decision making).

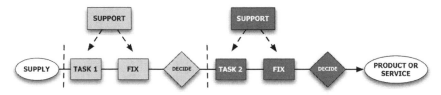

Depending on the factors of *technology*, *territory*, or *time*, these three could be combined into one unit, be divided between Supply and Production (combining Tasks 1 and 2), or remain as three separate entities.

The implications of the Tavistock principles are still profound for today's corporations. First, aligning boundaries with tangible outputs would reduce the number of boundaries in a process, cutting out much delay and waste. Second, individuals and teams organized within each boundary would have tangible results for which they could be held accountable. Third, the organization would have fewer units and functional entities to coordinate in completing a process.

Quality Process Design is something that never goes out of vogue in the corporate world. Specific methodologies for process design, monitoring process performance, and eliminating barriers may come and go. Titles and labels may change. Continuous improvement may yield new approaches, but the aim of Quality Process Design is to enable the organization to be perfectly designed to deliver what it promises to stakeholders.

Redesigning Ritz-Carlton's Housekeeping Process

As one example of a process (re)design that yielded high quality outputs, let's consider Ritz-Carlton's housekeeping process. As part of the company's overall approach to continuous improvement, one Ritz-Carlton property was assigned the lead for improving this process.

The Housekeeping Department is highly interdependent with Laundry, Engineering, Honor Bar, Room Service, Purchasing, Training, and other administrative functions. The project leader organized a cross-functional study team comprised of representatives from each of these departments to research the existing work process, recommend improvements, and monitor results. *(Notice how this cross-functional team aligns with the Survival Code principle #1: address key stakeholder needs. The entire project was derived from principle #2: the compelling purpose of the credo.)*

The study team was amazed to find how inefficient the apparently simple process was. In their process study, they found:

- The average time spent to clean a room was 28 minutes 9 seconds.
- Typically each room had 7.6 defects each day (a defect meaning something was either missing or faulty).
- The housekeeper traveled 525 feet (1/10 mile) to clean one room.
- The total annual cost of waste and rework for this process companywide was an estimated $458,000.

They documented exactly how much time each housekeeper devoted to the five primary housekeeping functions:

- Cleaning bathroom (37.2 percent)
- Making the bed (20 percent)
- Dust and restock (17.6 percent)
- Vacuum (8.9 percent)
- Strip room (8.6 percent)
- Other (7.8 percent)

The standard sequence for cleaning a room resulted in housekeepers retracing their steps many times (thus the 525 feet traveled). Invariably some small details (empty shampoo bottle, no pen, etc.) were overlooked. In addition, by examining the whole process, the team learned that servicing the Honor Bar created an additional interruption to the guest. Research showed the guests wanted few if any interruptions and short ones when they did occur.

The study team recommended organizing the housekeepers into small teams of three to clean each room. Here's how they divided up the work:

Person 1	Person 2	Person 3
Make bed	Make bed	Clean bath
Strip room	Dust room	Check closet
Restock room	Vacuum room	
Honor bar	Update status	

This team structure allowed them to combine steps, simplify the work flow, and eliminate time and distance traveled. For example Persons 1 and 2 made the bed while Person 3 cleaned the bathroom *(Survival Code #3: design high quality processes and #6: true partnerships).* The housekeepers were trained in routine maintenance tasks (fax machine maintenance, tub drain repair, light bulb replacement). This significantly reduced the calls to the engineering department—and eliminated additional guest disturbances *(Survival Code #4: solve problems at their source and #5: develop multi-skills).* Among the most noticeable improvements that emerged from the new process and team structure:

- Cycle time was reduced 65 percent. It took only 8 minutes to clean a room and stock the Honor Bar.
- Defects were cut 42 percent (4.3 vs. 7.6).
- Distance traveled was cut 64 percent to 209 feet.
- One guest interruption was eliminated (plus many other potential maintenance calls).
- The rooms were cleaner than before.
- The immediate savings to the company coming from all the above was $190,000; ongoing the annual savings were estimated to be over $300,000.
- Employee satisfaction increased dramatically. The pilot hotel was near the bottom of the company in employee satisfaction before the team system was introduced. After the change was made, the Housekeeping department moved to an 89.9 percent positive rating (#1 in the company).

Redesign efforts like these are conducted every year for every one of the 18 core processes. This is what the Survival Code principle #7 [adaptation] looks like in real life.

Redesigning US Synthetic's Manufacturing Process

If you were to visit the home office and manufacturing facility for US Synthetic (USS) in Orem, Utah, you might conclude this firm has nothing in common with a Ritz-Carlton hotel. The simply-appointed offices and the clean but fast-paced production facility are a far cry from the elegance and peaceful atmosphere in a Ritz-Carlton. Yet USS is also a leader in its industry. In 2011 it won the prestigious Shingo Prize for operational excellence (labeled by Business Week as "the Nobel Prize for manufacturing"), mirroring Ritz-Carlton's Baldrige Quality Awards in the service industry. USS makes an industrial Polycrystalline Diamond Cutter (PDC) for oil drilling equipment and is the dominant player in its industry. Over 30 percent of all oil drilling on this planet is done by bits with USS diamonds on them.

USS is the same company whose "Strategy Tree" we reviewed in Chapter 5. You will recall its vision is to improve the lives of employees, customers, shareholders and communities. In that respect it has much in common with Ritz-Carlton.

Growth has been one of the major challenges owner Louis Pope has faced in the 30 years of USS's operation. From its very humble beginnings, the company has grown to be a global company with 850 associates, but simply adding more people has not enabled the company to become a global standard of excellence. Like the Ritz-Carlton, USS relies on the innovative inputs from its associates to improve how it does business. In 2011 alone, more than 30,000 associates' improvement recommendations were implemented successfully.

One of the major improvements in recent years was an overhaul of the production process itself. The original production process followed traditional bureaucratic rules: keep the tasks divided up and closely supervised. The five primary production steps were grouped in separate departments: CG (Centerless Grinding), Height, Bonding, Chamfer, and Inspection. Raw materials moved slowly through the five departments as they were transformed into PDCs. It took approximately two weeks to produce PDCs in this process. As market demand for USS's products grew, each department usually purchased additional machines and hired more people to fill the void.

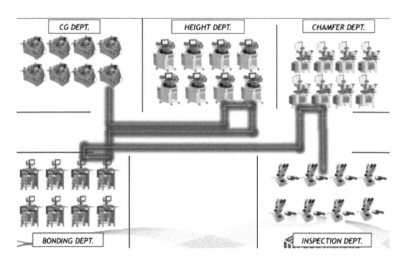

Then USS managers started learning Japanese methods for manufacturing excellence. *The Toyota Way* became their guide to improving their operation. Many associates were involved in redesigning the production process to bring together all five pieces of equipment and to organize their operators into "cells," self-sufficient production units. There are no handoffs in this new process. Each cell has all the resources it needs to make its product. Each of the 11 cells is named after a NASCAR motor speedway, identifying with a process and teamwork that produce incredible speed and quality. The new cells live up to their names. Today they produce a new PDC in about six hours!

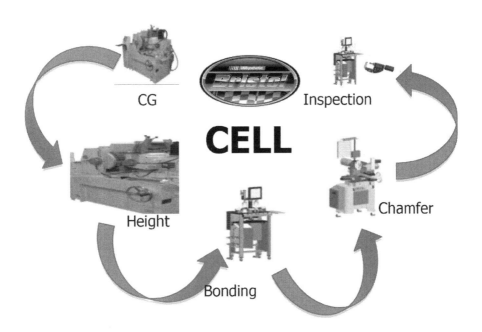

Designing Work Processes: A Summary

Designing your company to be aligned with the organizational survival code is both straightforward and complex. It is straightforward as it pursues the logical path we have explored thus far:

- Identify the most critical stakeholder needs that hold the keys to your survival (Chapter 5: Strategizing To Meet Stakeholder Needs).
- Align your strategic intent with those stakeholder needs (Chapter 6: Shape a Compelling Purpose).
- Design your work processes to deliver high quality results.

But the design of these core processes and their support systems can be complex. The few key steps reviewed in this chapter can make your efforts more effective, namely:

- Derive the core processes directly from your Purpose/ Strategy.
- Design each core process to be a Quality Process by removing unnecessary boundaries and barriers so that the work is free flowing and able to meet the stakeholders' needs. As we have seen with the Ritz-Carlton and US Synthetic examples, the same design principles can be applied in any industry.

We will explore the next steps in the following chapters. By now you are fully aware that designing an organization to survive and thrive in the marketplace requires a lot of time and energy from leaders and managers, but what could be more important to a corporation's survival than getting all of this right? If leaders aren't working on these things, what are they doing today that is more important?

These things are the "doughnut." Everything else is a "hole."

8
Solving Problems at Their Source

"No one has endeavored to carry out an enterprise where many hands were needed but has been well-nigh appalled at times at...the inability or unwillingness to concentrate on a thing and do it."

—*ELBERT HUBBARD*

"Our choicest plans have fallen through.
Our airiest castles tumbled over,
because of lines we neatly drew
and later neatly stumbled over."

— *PIET HEIN*

Organizations and other living systems are not immune from problems or catastrophes. When a volcano erupts or an earthquake triggers a destructive tsunami, the natural ecosystem is traumatized, but natural laws go to work and eventually restore order. These recuperative powers are driven by forces in nature. In a business enterprise, the recuperative powers must be driven by people, but human intellect sometimes comes into conflict with common sense. Here is one example:

> Some years ago, forest fires raged out of control near Laguna Beach, California. Though the National Guard had airplanes capable of dropping water on the blaze, none were mobilized until 19 hours after the first alert. Why? The head of the National Guard said, "We still do not know for sure who is in charge." Elsewhere the Marine Corps was willing to send volunteers, bulldozers, and water-dropping helicopters, but the local fire officials wouldn't take them because, "We have never drilled with them and they don't know our way of fighting fires." Meanwhile, 310 homes were being destroyed as the fire moved across the mountain.

What was it that blunted the instincts of these service providers to save lives and protect property? Why were organizational boundaries able to restrain highly trained professionals from their sworn duty to serve the citizens?

The answer lies in an organizational code that has been a blessing and a curse to organizations and their customers for centuries. This code is known as "bureaucracy" and is the template for most organizations in all corners of this planet.

The Bureaucratic Code

Centuries ago, enterprising managers experimented with ways to get more productivity from the combination of automated machinery and people. The Industrial Revolution began in Manchester, England and spread around the world. Years later, American Henry Ford perfected the assembly line, the most widely-adopted organizational innovation of the 20th century. Ford's original production process turned out one automobile every 13 hours. The assembly line produced one every 90 seconds. Efficiency specialists Frederick Winslow Taylor in the United States and Max Weber in Germany postulated organizational principles that managers could reapply to get similar results in their businesses. These principles have become known as the tenets of the bureaucratic organization.

What drives a bureaucracy? It's the assumption that *an organization is like a machine:* a collection of parts driven by a single control mechanism. For decades, organizations have sought alignment, order and control by following six basic rules:

1. **Task Specialization** *(job fragmentation)*–specialize tasks and reduce them to the smallest possible work cycle.

2. **Performance Standardization** *(find the one best way)*–do the work the same way every time. This is epitomized by the assembly line, but even administrative processes can be organized like an assembly line.

3. **Central Decision Making** *(unity of command)*–only those in authority should make decisions.

4. **Uniform policies** *(that's what the book says)*–treat all parts of the system alike.

5. **No duplication of functions** *(that's not my job)*–everyone does only their own job.

6. **Reward physical activity** *(the hired hand)*–pay a person only for physical labor and skills.

How have these six rules affected our society? Without question they have outperformed the agrarian society from whence they sprang. They have enabled us to mass-produce goods, thereby contributing to a higher standard of living for everyone. They do delineate job responsibilities across departments and up and down the hierarchy, and they drive out ambiguity. Unfortunately, the benefits of this organizational model have been steadily eroding over the past century. See if you can relate to this company's problem with bureaucracy:

A fertilizer plant ("Miller Inc.") was having serious safety problems. Work-related injuries were steadily increasing as manifested by recordable injuries and lost-time injuries. In the latest industry-wide report, the Miller plant was 11th out of 13 in recordable incidents rate. This track record was alarming to plant leadership. The plant manager commissioned a team of associates representing all levels and departments in the plant to diagnose the safety situation and recommend what needed to be done to establish "an injury-free work place."

One critical issue that emerged in the diagnosis was the identification and elimination of safety hazards. Here is the process they used with the responsible department listed in the middle column:

PROCESS STEP	DEPARTMENT	CHANGE OF STATE
1. Identify unsafe condition/hazard 2. Write Expenditure Request (ER) 3. ER authorized	Operations	**Write ER**
4. ER logged into computer	Accounting	
5. Group leader sets project priority 6. Assign to engineering 7. Assigned engineer logged into computer	Central Maintenance	
8. Investigate project 9. Determine workload	Engineering	

10. Scope job / write recommendation 11. Review / modify scope	Central Maintenance	**Write scope recommendation**
12. Accounting review	Accounting	
13. Finalize scope / estimate 14. Log estimate into computer	Central Maintenance	
15. ER approved	Operations	
16. Authorized budget logged into computer 17. Assign designer 18. Design project	Central Maintenance	**Design project**
19. Assemble materials 20. Schedule construction	Engineering	
21. Schedule reviews 22. Assign construction priority 23. Assign to engineering team	Central Maintenance	
24. Wait for shutdown	Operations	
25. Complete work	Engineering	**Complete work**
26. Update final cost on computer 27. Close job	Central Maintenance	
28. Final documentation	Accounting	

Looking at this process map, can you see why the plant had never eliminated a single hazard? The 28 steps went through the gauntlet of 14 handoffs once Operations had written an ER. I have noted in the right column the actual changes of state, or tangible outputs, that occurred in this process. The first tangible state change after identifying the hazard was when Operations wrote an Expenditure Request. This meant the good intention of a safe working environment was now degenerating into work. Thereafter, there were three additional tangible outputs: writing a recommendation of the project scope, designing the actual project to eliminate the hazard, and completing the project work. All other steps were in support or supervision of these few tangible outcomes.

The team now turned its attention to redesigning this important process. Using the principles reviewed in Chapter 7, they sought to eliminate steps and handoffs wherever possible. Here is the solution they eventually received approval for:

PROCESS STEP	DEPARTMENT	CHANGE OF STATE
1. Identify unsafe condition/ hazard 2. Write Expenditure Request (ER) 3. ER authorized	**Operations**	**Write ER**

4. Group leader sets project priority 5. Assign to engineering 6. Investigate project 7. Scope job/write recommendation	**Operations** (with Central Maintenance as needed)	**Write scope recommendation**
8. Review/modify scope 9. Finalize scope/estimate 10. ER approved 11. Assign designer 12. Design project	**Operations**	**Design Project**
13. Assemble materials 14. Schedule construction 15. Complete work 16. Final documentation and close job	**Operations** (with Central Maintenance as needed)	**Complete work**

Some steps were eliminated or consolidated, but the major change that was implemented was to assign all of these steps to Operations. How was this possible, given the complex technical skills that were required for the actual project design and implementation? The design team calculated that, with the number of such projects that needed to be accomplished, Operations was justified in having its own full-time engineer and a small maintenance project group. As a contingency, if the number of projects were to overwhelm the maintenance people assigned to Operations, Central Maintenance could be engaged to lend additional support. The Accountant assigned to Operations was given additional training and authorized by Central Accounting to approve and document all of the financials. (After all, the budget money in question was all Operations money!) Though this solution aligns with several Survival Code principles, the most obvious one is the new design enabled Operations to solve major safety problems at their source – on the production floor.

In the aftermath of this project, in the 12 months after hazards were actually eliminated and Operations was clearly accountable for its own safety performance, the Operations group (representing over 90 percent of the plant population) had zero recordable injuries…virtually "an injury-free work place!"

How to Solve Problems At Their Source

Let's now examine a few design principles that can enable your organization to solve problems at their source. The Miller Plant, along with some principles we covered in the previous chapter, will show you the way.

1. **Define process outputs as the fulfillment of stakeholder needs.** Bureaucracies often excel at fulfilling their own internal objectives rather than meeting the customers' or other stakeholders' needs. For instance, the Miller Plant might have had an objective of improving its safety record.

It could have improved its recordable injury rate to rank eighth on the list of 13 benchmark companies and met that objective, but aiming to have an injury-free workplace (most meaningful to the associates) transformed the process.

2. **Design free-flowing processes.** As we have seen in the Ritz-Carlton housekeeping, US Synthetic production, and Miller safety processes, reducing the number of process steps and the departmental handoffs can dramatically improve the process flow.

3. **Develop multi-skilled individuals.** Every process, regardless of the degree of automation, still relies on people to make it work and to solve any problems that arise. When a person working in a process has the necessary skills to address typical daily problems, these problems can be nipped in the bud.

This diagram (from my time at Procter and Gamble) shows the multi-skill roadmap for developing plant technicians.

- **Inner Circle:** Each team member was expected to become proficient at operating and solving daily problems on each piece of equipment on the production line.

- **Middle Circle:** Each team member had the opportunity to specialize through in-depth assignments in key support functions such as material preparation, technical troubleshooting, administrative reporting and quality control.

- **Outer Circle:** In addition, team members had the opportunity to lead team activities in critical areas – responsibilities that historically had been shouldered by managers and supervisors.

  This transparent roadmap revealed a career path that a person could move along over several years. As technicians moved in and out of different assignments and as several team members became skilled in all three circles, the production teams became experts in managing their own piece of the business and results exceeded many executives' fondest dreams. A corporate study, comparing the performance of these teams with teams in other plants that were organized along the bureaucratic lines of "one person/one job," revealed the multi-skilled teams had 25 percent better results in all production measures and in employee job satisfaction.

4. **Organize self-sufficient units.** The natural extension of the multi-skilled model is the creation of self-sufficient organizational units that, like the Miller Plant Operations, are able to handle daily issues with very few, if any, handoffs.

The primary unit of any department or function is the work team. The diagram here shows the tasks that one work team was responsible for in the course of making Pampers disposable diapers. Through P&G's multi-skill career path system, each team member became more competent and flexible in addressing any issue that might arise on the production floor. This team seldom needed specialists—at least one team member had already worked in each support area and could solve the team's problem immediately. Experience in coordinating the team's performance in cost savings, technical projects and supplier qualifications enabled the team to take initiative and improve its performance when new issues arose. Apply the same template to customer service departments, advertising teams, product development and accounting groups, and you will see similar results.

Other organizational units that might warrant the self-sufficient design model include business units, functional groups, business teams and special project teams. Each of these units should be designed to have all the needed resources available for their appointed strategy. (See the Vizir team example later in this chapter.)

5. **Invert the pyramid.** This phrase is often used to symbolize moving decision making to better engage lower levels in the organization. I take a slightly different view of this from a pure organization design perspective. If our aim is to solve problems at their source, then those who are closest to the problem should be qualified and enabled to make critical decisions. Those closest to the problem are the first line of defense. This might be the CEO for corporate strategic issues, a middle manager for managing a supplier relationship, or a team member for an accounting error. Inverting the pyramid enables the first line of defense to act

decisively. Obviously, for such a system to be practical, those first liners need to have the necessary skills, information, and authority to be able to make good, swift decisions.

When Problems Are Solved at Their Source

It seems only appropriate to conclude this chapter with some scenarios of how this principle of the survival code actually makes a difference at the bottom line. Solving problems at their source is a critical survival skill.

An airline employee working at a departure gate was trying to help her customers whose flight was delayed indefinitely due to bad weather conditions. All passengers were requested to remain in the gate area because their flight might be given the green light at any moment and would need to take off as soon as possible. As the situation dragged on, people began to be annoyed and weary. The gate agent wanted to purchase refreshments for her customers, but the catering manager told her this was against company policy. She wondered what she might do to help her customers, and then she realized that the airline at the neighboring gate was also a customer of her airline's catering services. She ordered the refreshments through the other airline and paid for them from her petty cash fund. Her customers were pleased and, in the spirit of the inverted pyramid, the catering manager was instructed by the company CEO that his responsibility in such a situation was to help the gate attendant solve the problem, not to blindly recite company policy. This thinking was a driving force in the airline's turnaround from near bankruptcy to market leadership in a few short years.

One family came to the **Boston Ritz-Carlton** to celebrate several events at Sunday brunch. After helping the family pile out of their van, the doorman noticed a large pool of oil spreading from underneath the vehicle. Inspecting things more closely, he determined the oil plug had recently fallen out. Getting a colleague to cover his spot, he retraced the van's path with the driver until he found the oil plug. Returning to the hotel, he made arrangements to have the plug replaced and fresh oil installed. "It will be taken care of," he told the guest. "Enjoy your brunch!" The driver joined the family celebration after a mere 15-minute delay. No wonder Ritz-Carlton has a higher occupancy rate than the hotel industry average.

A warehouse technician noticed that a large supermarket chain had recently stopped ordering one of his company's flagship products. He called a contact at the supermarket's distribution center and asked if there was a problem. "Yes," his contact replied. "Your new pallets don't fit the layout of our facilities. Your pallets are larger than all the others and mess up our neat rows. Our fork truck drivers are complaining about the extra clearance they have to give your pallets." After the call, the technician asked his colleague to cover his duties for him while he visited the distribution center. There he saw and photographed exactly what the problem was. He went back to the plant, arranged to resize the pallets and won approval from the supermarket chain to restock the product in its stores. A major source of corporate revenue was restored.

Procter & Gamble's business team was responsible for strategy and pan European execution of Vizir, the innovative liquid laundry detergent that is known today as Liquid Tide in the U.S. P&G organized business teams for each of its big brands in Europe. The teams' organizational structure looked like this:

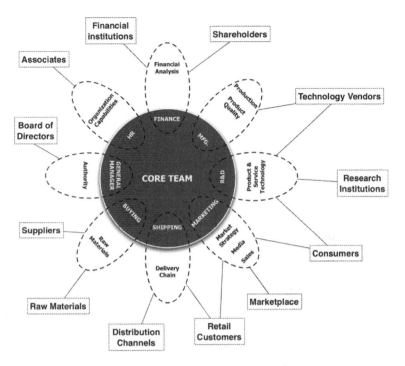

Each team was led by one of the European country's general managers. Team members represented the functions that were critical to strategizing and rolling out the brand across Europe. The functional team members depicted here were chosen to provide access, if needed, to any company resources (examples are in the "petals" of the diagram) and any external stakeholders (those connected to the petals from the outside). When an unseasonal monsoon and a severe drought both hit the Philippines one summer, that country's coconut crop (90 percent of the world's supply) was decimated. Coconut oil, a key ingredient in Vizir, skyrocketed in price overnight and wiped out the entire profit margin on the brand.

The business team called an emergency meeting. All team members came together in the plant where Vizir was produced and examined the problem from a 360° view. All cost elements were studied to see what might be adjusted in formula, packaging, marketing, manufacturing and distribution. At the end of one business day, the team had identified short-term cost savings that restored the original unit profit margin and longer-term savings that would advance profits even more. The general manager got approval from European and Company Management to make the needed changes, and team members collaborated to make the changes swiftly. In a matter of a few weeks, Vizir was in the black again.

These four vignettes illustrate the power of solving problems at their source. Customers are soothed through a major inconvenience. A special occasion remains special despite a car problem. A flagship product is back on the store shelves. A brand's profitability is restored quickly in response to natural calamities. All this, not because of executive actions, but because some associates were capable and authorized to solve the problem on the spot. Bureaucracy's rules, which surely existed in each of these situations, were countermanded by a survival instinct in people that mirrored that of natural ecosystems.

Changing Mindsets to Survive

The Organizational Survival Code requires some profound mindset shifts from the bureaucratic code. Some of these shifts include:

- Moving beyond performance standardization to being driven by purpose and strategy.
- Moving beyond task specialization to thinking of all tasks as part of a process.
- Moving beyond efficiency to self-sufficiency.
- Moving beyond hierarchical thinking to thinking functionally.
- Moving beyond narrow spans of control to control at the point of action.

As we have seen in this chapter, upgrading some of our organizational beliefs can drive an alignment with the survival code that yields new life amidst the sea of change.

9
Thriving on Complexity

"Business...leaders must realize that globalization,
virtualization, competition
and transparency will change most aspects of most business
sectors in almost all countries and regions."

— *JOHN MAHONEY*

"In the future, there will be 'mass customization...
Products and services will be mass produced
and customized for each individual customer."

—*STANLEY M. DAVIS*

A consultant once gave clients this counsel: "When it comes to doing things better, faster or cheaper, you can choose any two, but you can't be strong in all three." What if your survival as a corporation depends on being strong in all three? What then?

Today's global economy, as John Mahoney points out, is a complex one that throws a steady stream of ever-changing demands at business enterprises. The leadership and organizational skills required today are much more complex than the requirements of our predecessors. More often than not, survival isn't a matter of doing A or B or C, but doing A *and* B *and* C. In the previous chapter, we noted that bureaucracy has become misaligned with today's global marketplace because it is focused and tightly structured, but not flexible or adaptive enough. In this chapter, we are going to explore the survival code principle of complexity and see how organizations can be shaped to be focused, structured *and* adaptive.

Complexity in Nature

Complexity (e.g., systems develop more complex, specialized functions over time) is one part of the survival code that is not well understood. For years I had misrepresented this principle when teaching it in workshops. I (and workshop participants) translated those words "complex" and "specialized" into the embodiment of bureaucracy – narrow, specialized departments throwing up boundaries to break up a work process coupled with layer upon layer of hierarchy micromanaging everything below them. What my colleagues and I were missing is that complexity is one of the factors that allows an organization to survive, not move it toward extinction. Our error was ascribing modern organizational meanings to natural systems dynamics.

One of my favorite pictures clearly illustrates the principle of complexity in living systems. The picture is of a mother grizzly bear catching a fish in the middle of a river. Standing off to the side are her two cubs, watching mama's every move. These two young "systems" are learning more complex and specialized skills to enable their survival. You see, the natural law of survival requires that the system develop more complex and specialized skills to handle whatever the environment might throw at it. Instead of segmenting skills and piling on layers of supervision, complexity in nature is all about *expanding* skills and *reducing* the need for external supervision. One day, the bear cubs will not need mama to survive. They will be self-sufficient in handling changing weather patterns, migrating food sources, attacks from other animals and civilization encroaching on their territory. They will be able to fit into the ecological order of things, maintain their steady state and solve problems as they occur without any bailouts!

Complexity and Organizational Survival

Complexity in nature refers to a system (or being) that develops more complex and specialized skills so it can adapt to its changing environment. We have seen how Apple started as a computer company in a California garage, but today sells a host of products all over the world. Apple's team has been challenged to develop more complex and specialized skills in its 37 years of economic fluctuations, technical ups and downs, and global organizational challenges.

Walmart, the retail juggernaut that strikes fear into present and would-be competitors, failed miserably in its attempts to establish a business in Germany. After some years of consistent disappointments, Walmart sold its 80 plus German stores to a competitor and withdrew from the market. Yet Walmart has an enormous, thriving business in Mexico. Mastering one's business in a variety of foreign cultures is another complex challenge for any company.

People Express, the first company to earn $1 billion by its fifth year of existence, became totally overwhelmed by the complexity of managing the systems required by a sudden increase in the number of routes, by different types of aircraft, and an exploding number of customers. The more successful they were, the more overwhelmed they became by the consequences of their success. CEO Don Burr once said, "I'm not concerned about complexity. Any time you have six people in your organization, you already have a complex situation." Sadly, as Burr learned, complexity does have different faces and can require a plethora of adaptations from a corporation. Communications, work processes, systems, associate engagement, customer loyalty, supplier partnerships – all are complex in today's world. Fall short in even a couple of critical areas and your firm may go down.

All of this speaks to the criticality of developing a breadth of skills and judgment that can make your company self-sufficient in the market's perfect storm. In this chapter, I will explore a few organization design tools that can increase your level of natural complexity by enhancing self-sufficiency.

Getting Information to the Point of Action

A corollary to the survival code principle of "solve problems at their source" is the maxim: "get information to those who need to take action based upon it." When people in different parts of an organization have the same information, they tend to make the same decisions. I have seen this in many situations. Therefore, if we want people to solve problems at the source, we need to ensure they have the relevant information to make sound problem-solving decisions.

How do you know who requires what information? Follow the work process. What do the various associates have to *do* in the process? What information do these associates require for the process to remain *free flowing*? Here's an example of the information needs for a printing services work process:

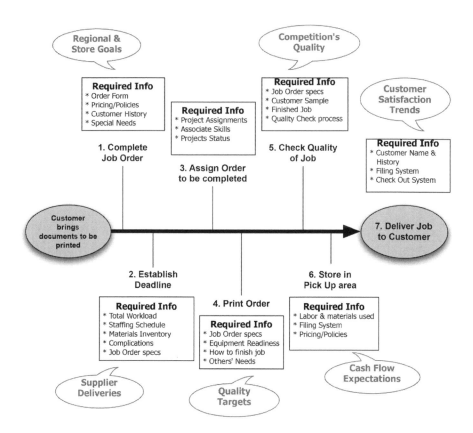

The work process begins with a customer bringing in a job to be printed. There are seven steps required to deliver the finished product back to the customer. For each step, note the information that the person/persons need to keep their part of the process free flowing and defect free. The gray clouds represent information from the hierarchy or external stakeholders that everyone in the process needs to understand; the rectangular boxes contain internal information from upstream or downstream in the process.

As this illustration shows, the Information system needs to be designed to consider:

- **Top-Down, Bottom-Up needs:** Company goals, policies, expectations from the top down; actual data about quality, efficiency, skill levels and financial accounting generated by the process from the bottom up.
- **Lateral information needs:** Upstream/downstream, internal customer/supplier data and communication.
- **Outside-In and Inside-Out needs:** Suppliers, end users, and competitors' standards that affect your customers' expectations.

Some previous design choices should provide valuable inputs to the Information system. The Balanced Scorecard should tell you what the most important results are and how well you are delivering against them. The Stakeholder Feedback System should tell you what is important to key stakeholders. The Quality Process Design should identify who needs to do what tasks in the process. The boundary choices and structure should identify which associates are responsible for problem solving at each step. (Without going into great detail, let me merely point out that by using the Quality Process Design approach outlined in Chapter 8 for this print shop situation, all seven steps could be done by one person, with some team rotation at the front desk assuring constant attention there. Before too long, every member of the print shop would be competent in all tasks and would have all relevant information for priority setting and decision making.)

The principle here is a departure from the way most information systems are approached. Rather than designing information to go first to the top, design it to go primarily to the point of action.

Cross-Functional Career Paths

This is a variation on the theme of multi-skilled work roles. Rather than gain experience in everything in one function, gain some significant experiences in multiple functions. This is particularly important in the development of higher levels of management or general management.

Typically, associates in subunits that interface with each other have a hard time appreciating each other's situation. Working for a time on the other side of the line not only creates natural empathy for each other, but also develops the knowledge and perspective for solving interface misalignments that steal time and money from the bottom line. The closer one moves to general management, the more important it is to really understand all that goes on in the various functions of the business.

At Procter & Gamble, for instance, those in Brand Management all have an assignment early in their careers to work as part of the sales force. This helps them understand how their marketing campaigns actually play out in the retail market. Managers in Manufacturing, Product Development, and Finance may have an assignment on an Advertising Brand

Team to give them experience working with other functions and to see how everything comes together in the business.

Similarly, one of the requirements for new Ritz-Carlton managers is to operate at the front desk for several months because the front desk is connected to all other functions. When these managers leave the front desk and focus on their new role in Housekeeping or Catering, they take with them the experience and knowledge of how all the functions are interdependent in serving the guests.

There are no limits to the combinations that come from a cross-functional career path system: accountants working in manufacturing, engineers working in product development, chemists working in manufacturing labs, general managers having worked in several functions and so forth. In all cases, these moves can develop the individuals' complex skills that can be applied to whatever challenges the marketplace may serve up in the future. However, this rotation of assignments should be planned carefully in terms of duration and level of activity so that the experiences truly multiply the individuals' skills and business perspectives. Rotation programs that merely place individuals on a merry-go-round to punch a checklist don't always build greater self-sufficiency.

Expanding Skills of Supervisors

Another facet of building complex, specialized skills applies to the work of management. As one builds up the self-sufficiency of a work team, this frees up supervisor capacity to do other things.

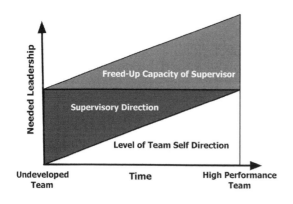

Harvard professors Richard Walton and Len Schlesinger introduced this model to illustrate the dynamics of team development. As teams develop greater competencies and stronger teamwork, much of the direction provided in the earlier stages by supervisors can be supplied now by team members. Self-sufficient teams free up the supervisor's capacity to do other things, but what is a supervisor supposed to do—especially in tough economic times and with executives' propensity to downsize the workforce?

Those who simply eliminate supervisory or managerial positions may be missing some great opportunities to add value to the system. The Tavistock Institute researchers ran into this very dynamic more than 50 years ago; it is nothing new. The Tavistock people use the term "Boundary Management" to express a value-adding enhancement to supervision. Boundary management means managers add the most value not by supervising what goes on *inside* the team/unit, but by working on performance issues *between* the team/unit and its various interfaces (i.e., poor quality materials from suppliers, equipment design with vendors, aligning sales campaigns with retailers, etc.). These issues often "fall through the cracks," adding enormous waste, rework and cost to the system. Make this simple analysis with your organization's teams or departmental groups and you will be amazed at what you find:

- Map out the various interface groups with whom the team/ department interacts.
- For each interface, list any breakdowns or problems because of something being misaligned.
- Identify the financial cost of these breakdowns or deviations.
- Assign the appropriate individuals (supervisors? managers?) to address these issues.

After these four steps have been completed, you will find the company has simplified its work and saved an enormous amount of money—far more money than if the corporation had downsized all of the supervisors!

W. Edwards Deming used to sum up the principle of Boundary Management this way, "Managers work *on* the system, not *in* the system." This design principle is not only for manufacturing teams or processes. It can add value to any endeavor in a corporation.

Building Lateral Collaboration

The term "lateral capabilities" was first coined by Jay Galbraith, one of the great organization design thinkers of our day. These capabilities enable people in different organizational units to add flexibility, responsiveness, and collaboration to bureaucracy's clear lines of accountability. We call this "filling in the white spaces" in the organization chart—working laterally between the so-called silos that often characterize a bureaucracy.

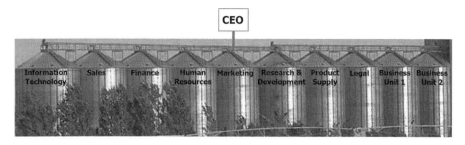

As Galbraith, Downey and Kates point out in their book, *Designing Dynamic Organizations,* there are a number of design tools that build lateral capability. These tools range from informal, natural choices to more structured, designed solutions. The following diagram illustrates the complexity of these collaborative tools. The tools become more complex as one moves from bottom to top.

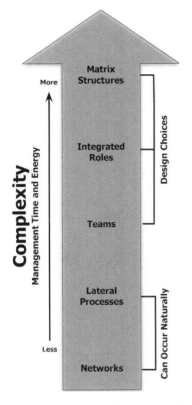

■   **Networks** are informal groups that come together in places such as annual meetings, communities of practice, training classes and internet bulletin boards or chat rooms. They connect people who normally don't have contact. Some corporations design such events with enough unscheduled time to encourage networking.

■   **Lateral processes** are specific work agreements between two units. For example, Finance and Marketing might define the process by which they will work together during the annual budgeting ritual. This process might include agreement on the start and end of the process, objectives, division of responsibility, commitment of resources, timetables and milestones, etc. (See more about such processes in chapter 10 when I discuss Partnership Commitments). Such agreements provide structure and accountability to the needed flexibility when working between silos.

■ **Teams** are more formal and structured than networks. They can be formed by project or by special issues (i.e., quality teams, innovation teams, execution teams).

Multifunctional business teams, such as the Vizir brand team mentioned in Chapter 8, have proven to be effective tools for integrating all functions and areas of expertise required to manage a business unit. All interdependent functions are represented on the core team, whose major tasks are to shape the business unit's strategy and coordinate the execution to reach the targeted results. The work of such a team is mostly analytical and conceptual. The actual execution is handled daily by the individual functions. But the multifunctional team adds value by aligning all the individual efforts to increase speed, reduce errors and find more innovative solutions. A well-designed business team has representation from all functions involved in the business' output. Collectively, the representatives can assemble all needed experience and expertise to analyze the competitive situation and deliver innovative solutions faster than moving up and down the silos.

■ **Integrative roles** enable one person to bring together different silos for specific purposes. For example, a Talent Development manager might be given responsibility to coordinate talent development in several functions to ensure consistency throughout the company. Or one manager responsible for both sales and marketing might be able to get the two functions to collaborate better.

■ **Matrix Structures** are the most complex and oft misunderstood lateral capabilities tools and therefore will be addressed in more detail below.

The Misunderstood Matrix Structure

Matrix structures were invented in the aerospace industry because the typical silo bureaucracy was unable to respond/ adjust fast enough to rapidly changing market dynamics. A matrix structure brings together different functional experts into one business unit or team to collaborate in building the business.

I encounter the matrix tool in nearly every organization I consult with, but find too few managers who actually understand the principles behind the matrix structure.

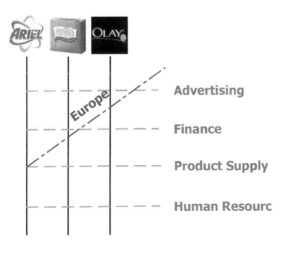

This graphic shows a typical matrix structure in the 21st century, a more elaborate version from its predecessors. I will use my alma mater, Procter & Gamble, to illustrate the matrix dynamics. The matrix maps out relationships between Business Units (in this example Ariel laundry detergent, Pampers disposable diapers, and Olay skin care); Corporate Functions (Advertising, Finance, Product Supply, Human Resources); and Geographical Regions (Europe in this example). Solid lines mean direct accountability; dotted lines symbolize support or advisory responsibilities.

Those accustomed to bureaucracy's clean lines of authority become uncomfortable with the idea of two lines converging on one person or unit. The question of who has the solid line and who has the dotted line becomes a hotly debated topic in many corporations. Generally, the debate should be settled by answering this question: with which unit do you want the associate to identify? If it is important that he/she identify fully with the BU team, then that should be the solid line. If, on the other hand, an associate must give priority to his/her professional responsibility to provide an unbiased perspective in the BU, then the solid line might be better with the function, even though the person may be working exclusively in the BU.

Dissatisfied players attempt to expand their power and control in the matrix, leading to the frequent complaints I hear such as, "responsibilities are unclear," "decision making authority is a source of contention" and "associates are confused about whose directives they should follow." Such statements are symptomatic of those not understanding basic matrix principles. Here are a few rules of engagement that should be operating in a matrix structure.

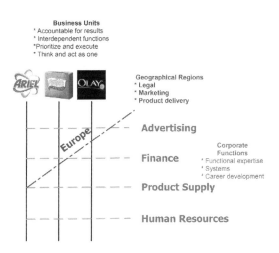

Business Units
* Accountable for results
* Interdependent functions
*Prioritize and execute
* Think and act as one

Geographical Regions
* Legal
* Marketing
* Product delivery

Advertising

Finance

Corporate Functions
* Functional expertise
* Systems
* Career development

Product Supply

Human Resources

1.   The   Business Units   (BUs)   are typically   the   profit centers and accountable for the business results. Functional resources are assigned to the BU to apply their expertise to the business needs. The intent is for the Business Unit team to think and act as one and have all the needed resources, yielding better and faster execution. (In other words, being self-sufficient to fulfill its accountability.)

2. **The Corporate Functions** play a very different, but critical role in the matrix. How does the organization ensure that the functional resources in the BUs have the right expertise? How does it avoid creating unnecessary complexity by doing common tasks very differently in each BU? Who looks after the career interests of functional professionals assigned to Pampers today? These are all issues that the Functions should manage in a matrix. The Functions are the

developers of each person's technical expertise, the keepers of the common functional systems and the mentors and orchestrators of the professionals' careers who are in their functional discipline.

3. **The Geographical Region.** The global market has driven this additional dimension of the structure. Somewhere in the blend of BUs and Corporate Functions is the additional need to tailor the operation to unique needs of a Geographical Region of the world. Despite the many commonalities of today's global market, there are still cultural differences, legal differences and large distances to be managed. The principal regional role is to manage product delivery, marketing executions and legal requirements that are unique to the local area. Obviously, the Regional organization must partner with the BUs and the Functions to make everything come together.

The word *partner* is the key ingredient in the matrix. The three legs of the matrix are interdependent in the operation of the business. The structure is designed to keep everyone's attention on the doughnut—to stimulate dialogue, examination of business issues from multiple viewpoints, and synergistic problem solving. The matrix is designed to examine the needs of both long-term AND short-term, of individual AND organizational development, of unique AND standard solutions. If one side always wins any of these debates, you don't really have a matrix despite what you might call the structure. On the other hand, if this true teamwork exists in the company culture, it makes little difference who has the solid line and who has the dotted line.

The complaints I hear about the matrix are all traceable to ineffective partnership relationships. Instead of adhering to the neat roles outlined here, organizations experience some or all of the following dynamics:

- BUs and/or Geographical Regions refuse to adopt a Corporate Functional system because "our needs are different."
- Corporate Functions unilaterally impose a corporate system on BUs that is financially or logistically impractical.
- Regions attempt to manage their market as a profit center and clash with the BU in the process.
- BUs refuse to consider transferring a person because of "the needs of the business" even though that person needs (and deserves) a broader assignment.
- Corporate Functions attempt to downsize or cut costs in order to "improve their numbers" to the CEO—without consulting the BUs.

You get the picture–well-meaning people being distracted by the doughnut holes. Without true partnership relationships, the matrix can be a complex and frustrating structure in which to work. Managers that are used to the crisp, precise responsibilities in a bureaucracy and who thrive in a "command and control" system will be frustrated daily in a matrix. This is one of the reasons why Galbraith et al. place it at the top of the lateral capabilities options in terms of complexity and management energy required.

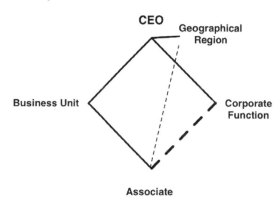

There is one piece of the matrix structure that I have not yet addressed. It is also an element that many corporations do not address.

As this diagram shows, the CEO (or division president or general manager) is an essential ingredient in a matrix, especially if the key leaders are new to the team or organization. If the three legs of the matrix cannot come to agreement on how to proceed with cost cutting, or associate career development, or marketing campaigns, someone must be able to resolve the stalemate. Thus, the essential role of tie-breaker and final decision maker falls to the CEO. In time, the three groups and their leaders may be able to engage in synergistic dialogue and solutions, but a release valve (final decision maker) is needed if all else fails.

Conclusion: Thriving on Complexity

In this chapter we have explored the possibilities an organization has to address because of the increasingly complex demands made upon it by a global marketplace. Those who can meet the challenge of complexity will survive. Those who fall short will probably fade from view in a few years. Meeting the challenge of complexity means you have self-sufficient individuals and units that have the requisite resources, structure and flexibility to respond better than your competitors to changing market demands. The tools reviewed here can help you have the right resources in the right place working together as required:

- Getting relevant information to the point of action increases a person's ability to make the right decisions and solve problems at their source.

- Pursuing multi-functional career assignments gives key associates even more skills and perspectives to understand, strategize, collaborate and solve the most complex problems quickly and effectively.

- Expanding the skills of supervisors/managers to address boundary interface issues enables an organization to increase its effectiveness exponentially.

- Increasing lateral collaboration between business units, functions and geographies can institutionalize the high degree of partnership that will make a substantial difference in adaptation and extending your organization's lifecycle.

10
Developing Synergistic Partnerships

"Some people seek to get. They seek money, power, or prestige. With persistence and luck they might obtain what they seek. Some people seek to give. They want to provide opportunities, growth, and independence for others. Whether they are lucky or not, they will be able to obtain what they seek. They will find opportunities to help people grow.

…When 'getters' get what they want, it is usually at others' expense. The human costs are almost always heavy. When 'givers' get what they want, others prosper with them…Only to them does allegiance flow without expense of energy on their part. People want to work with them and for them."

—*C. TERRY WARNER*

"An institution is like a tune. It is not constituted by individual sounds,
but by the relations between them."

— PETER DRUCKER

In the previous two chapters I built a case for developing self-sufficient individuals and organizational units in your company. Now we will turn our attention to developing synergistic partnerships. "What?" you may say, "first we are supposed to be self-sufficient and now we are supposed to partner with outsiders?" Yes! It's not a matter of self-sufficiency *or* partnerships. Today's global market requires both. Synergistic partnerships actually extend your influence (therefore increasing your self-sufficiency) in the stakeholder ecosystem in which you operate.

Principles and Tools of Synergy

The natural law of synergy says the whole is greater than the sum of its parts. A corollary to this law is: trying to optimize each part singularly will suboptimize the whole. Tracing the roots of the related word *synergism*, we find these elements:

Syn — similar, alike, aligned

Erg — a unit of work or energy

Ism — bound together by a common factor

From this definition, we understand that synergy isn't created by *adding* things together; it comes from *binding* things together *differently*. It isn't necessarily the number of resources you have that is critical, or the value of each individual item, but the way in which everything comes together. This explains why one organization reduces its associate enrollment and sees no gains in productivity or profitability while another does the same and not only increases profitability, but actually builds trust as well.

For example, as Procter & Gamble's business evolved in Europe, new technology and changing market conditions made some manufacturing locations obsolete. The Newcastle City Road Plant, part of P&G since the early 1950s, was targeted to be closed. This meant its 250 employees were to be transferred to other locations or laid off.

Plant manager Tony Turnbull, quoting former CEO Richard R. Deupree, said to his leadership team, "If we truly believe, 'our employees' interests are inseparable with the company's interests,' then how do we handle the fact that we are closing the plant?" The employees' need was to have a job, the leaders reasoned, so the leaders' job was to see they were well placed. P&G set up an out-placement office in the plant. Managers used company time to counsel those who were leaving. They personally visited other employers, offering to let them look through employee personnel files and interview employees in the P&G facility.

In the end, all employees were matched with good jobs in the area and their sentiment to the leaders was, "We wish we were staying with P&G, but you can be proud of your company – you have done it the Procter Way."

Tony Turnbull changed P&G's relationship with several stakeholders to actually build trust in what most would have called a no-win situation.

The key point for competing in the global market is *to change the nature of your relationships—how you work together with your stakeholders*. In this chapter we will review some personal and organizational principles that can enable you to develop synergistic partnerships.

Being a Partner

Some time ago a large company (let's call it Alpha) took out a full-page advertisement in a newspaper. It opened with this sentence: *"We'd like to thank our best suppliers worldwide."* Then 152 suppliers were recognized as Alpha's Suppliers of the Year. At the bottom of the page, the final sentence read: *"Working together to achieve customer enthusiasm with exciting Alpha products."*

The casual reader might have been impressed with this company's recognition of its best suppliers, but those who knew the background smiled at the advertisement's irony. Just two years before this recognition, Alpha had torn up its contracts with many of these suppliers and demanded the terms be renegotiated with significant across-the-board price reductions. During this episode, one of Alpha's suppliers asked me, "How do we know they won't do the same thing six months from now? They tore up a legal contract and made us bid lower. They could do it again. They've destroyed our trust in them."

Despite their resentment, this company and most of Alpha's other suppliers swallowed hard and lowered their prices, but the suppliers compensated in their own way as one of them explained, "I can tell you how we and everyone else will make up some of the loss. We'll lower the quality of our materials." Later I read where an industry observer stated, "I don't know of any major supplier who will take a new design to Alpha today, because, in the end, they will give it to the lowest bidder."

Notice how committed these "partners" are to "working together to achieve customer enthusiasm with exciting Alpha products." What was the bottom line of this situation? Did the cost savings from supplier contracts and the full-page ad actually help Alpha's business? Short term, Alpha did save millions of dollars, but its position in today's marketplace continues to decline because customer perceptions are unchanged about its poor product quality and Alpha's senior management is still desperately trying to squeeze out more profits.

Calling yourself a partner does not make you one. That's why the first principle for developing synergistic partnerships is *being* a partner. Your character, your values, your code of conduct for your life – your very being – must be anchored in working for the mutual benefit of others. "Everyone you work with is a partner," said Saturn Corporation president Skip LeFauve. "You can achieve so much more if you treat them like one." As he guided Saturn's startup phase, Skip was able to create synergistic partnerships with the local UAW bargaining unit, 9,000 team members who all came from other General Motors locations, a network of hundreds of retail dealerships across the United States, and thousands of Saturn owners. At the peak of its success in 1994, Saturn was the third highest selling car model in the U.S.

What might you achieve if, instead of a relationship of win-lose exchanges, you had real partners who volunteered their best resources (financial, people, technical innovation, services, ideas) to help you when you really needed them? Here are two more leaders who developed a true partnership with great results.

In the late 1980s Walmart chairman Sam Walton and Procter & Gamble CEO John Smale agreed to better align their business systems with each other in the belief that it would improve the bottom line for both companies. To initiate the improvements, P&G managers from advertising, information services, logistics, sales, manufacturing, distribution, and finance moved their families from Cincinnati, Ohio (P&G's hometown) to Bentonville, Arkansas (Walmart's headquarters). They formed a task force with their Walmart counterparts. Their charge was simple: study how we each do business and develop totally aligned systems to better serve the consumers who buy P&G products in Walmart stores.

It seemed to be a straightforward proposition, but manufacturers and retailers in the consumer products industry historically have competed with each other for profit margins. How could the unspoken competitive juices between P&G and Walmart be eliminated in this critical project?

At 8:02 a.m. on the new team's first workday, through the door came "Mr. Sam" Walton himself—unannounced and unexpected! Noting all the offices were empty, he asked the receptionist, "Where are the P&G folks? I want to welcome them to our team." He was told they weren't in yet; all were at the bank trying to cut through red tape related to their home mortgages. It seems the local bank was hesitant to approve mortgage loans for so many out-of-towners.

Sam immediately called the bank and said, "Hello, this is Sam Walton. I understand some of our partners from Procter & Gamble are having trouble with their mortgages. These people are my business partners. Is there anything we can do to expedite their loans?" Not surprisingly, every loan was quickly approved!

Those who knew Sam Walton will tell you this episode was "typical Sam." His behavior revealed how seriously he took this new partnership. As far as he was concerned, there were no boundaries separating Walmart and P&G: their business was his business. Sam Walton's win-win thinking laid the groundwork for a win-win partnership.

One of the P&G managers on the team told me, "Each of us was so impressed that Sam would go out of his way to help us and to make us feel like we were all on the same team. He motivated us to really look out for each other's interests." From that day forward the managers from the two companies truly worked together for the same end. They made many changes that, though not ideal for either company's existing systems, did a better job of fulfilling the consumers' needs. Marketing plans and product promotions between the two companies were tightly coordinated to present a more timely, unified message to consumers. Shipping systems were aligned to make it easier and safer to move products through the entire pipeline. Information systems were simplified to allow for faster tracking and reporting.

These improvements enabled the combined P&G-Walmart organization to deliver a box of Tide or a tube of Crest toothpaste from the production plant to the store shelf with the highest quality, lowest cost, and fastest time ever. The more efficient pipeline cut warehouse inventories in half, freeing up capital for both partners. Part of the cost savings was passed on to the consumer, yielding a lower purchase price than competition could offer. In the twelve months after the new system was operating, the volume of P&G products sold in Walmart stores was up 50 percent! Both partners won big with the new system.

The hidden ingredient in this partnership was the mutual trust the two CEOs passed along to their associates. John Smale moved some of his key managers to the partner's headquarters. Sam Walton made it his business to help the Cincinnatians establish their homes and working relationships in Bentonville. Synergistic partnerships don't begin by people doing different things. Such partnerships begin by the key players *being* trustworthy partners.

Committing to Each Other's Success

For years, my wife Charlee and I have organized leadership workshops on whitewater rafting expeditions. The workshop topics and the physical realities of the rafting experience make for a powerful learning laboratory. One of the early lessons every rafting team learns is the reality of "we are all in the same boat." Someone in the back of the raft cannot say to those in front, "You have a problem up there. We will wait while you straighten the nose of the boat." Before long, on every rafting trip, the entire team is committed to each other's success and will do whatever the river guide commands them to do to keep the boat afloat.

The reality of "we are all in the same boat" is just as real in a business enterprise as it is on the river. A synergistic partnership requires this kind of commitment to work and sacrifice for each other's well-being, recognizing that we are taking care of ourselves at the same time we are taking care of our partners.

A great example of this comes from Skip LeFauve's relationship with the Saturn retailers. True to his beliefs, Skip felt Saturn could achieve so much more if it treated the retail dealers as business partners. In Saturn language, these outside agencies were all called retailers (not dealers). Once a business became a Saturn retailer, its leaders were invited to Spring Hill,

Tennessee to go through the Saturn Team Member Orientation. The values of customer service, quality of product and teamwork were applied to a retail unit as well as to a production team. Skip LeFauve organized regular meetings with the retailer network to update each other on what was happening in the Saturn world and to find ways to help each other.

In one network meeting in 1993 Saturn retailers wanted to know how soon the Spring Hill facility would be going to a third production shift. "We never have enough cars," lamented one retailer. "We have sold out all of the cars on our lot. The only test drive car we have is my own personal car. Then, our customers have to wait weeks to take delivery of their car."

Skip replied that General Motors would not allow them to start a third shift until Saturn was in the black financially. "We are right on track with our commitment to GM, but it will take us another year to get there."

A retailer asked, "How much money do you need to get into the black?"

"About $13 million," Skip replied.

After doing some quick calculating of annual sales, the retailer stated, "That's about $140 per car, or 1 percent of the sales price. If we rebate back to you $140 per car, can we get our third shift?"

Skip readily agreed and passed the word up the line to GM leadership. The third shift was organized, sales volume accelerated accordingly, and the 1 percent voluntary retailer rebate moved Saturn into the black one year ahead of projections. The commitment to help each other succeed paid off for both partners.

Aligning Daily Priorities

The goodwill that partners generate with their good intentions often dissipates in the heat of the daily business battle. Things don't go as planned, people scramble around to respond appropriately and sometimes the partnership efforts become disjointed and even at odds with one another, creating a need for business partners to refocus their priorities and realign their actions. One of my clients ("Pharma") had developed its strategy and was anxious to accelerate progress toward its endpoints. Key leaders in all of the Pharma's development functions came together in a workshop to create an integrated action plan to fulfill their strategy. Here is the process they employed over a four-day period:

Step 1: Identify personal actions that will help fulfill the organization's strategy. The content of Pharma's strategy was broken down into 16 categories, such things as creating future medicines, meeting key stakeholder needs (patients, providers, payers, etc.), ensuring quality, global teamwork, etc. Each manager identified the few categories in which he/ she could add the most value in the coming year and selected three to six actions to pursue further.

Step 2: Align personal actions within the function. Small functional groups came together to give each other feedback on their initial priorities. Each individual learned from peers: a) which priorities they felt offered the highest strategic benefits, b) which priorities embodied the function's strengths and c) which priorities (or sub-points) needed attention because they weren't aligned with the strategy, needed modification or didn't seem to fit within the function's charter.

Step 3: Derive the highest priorities from the personal actions. Using the feedback from step 2, individuals re-examined their actions according to potential benefit and degree of difficulty. They chose three to six priorities to work on further.

Step 4: Shape the priorities into a personal action plan. Individuals produced an action plan with three to six specific actions mapped out to show:

    a. The action to be taken.

    b. The reason this action is strategically important.

    c. Opportunities to be seized or obstacles to be removed.

    d. Specific steps to be taken by specific deadlines.

e. Resources required (people, money, time, etc.).

f. Expected measurable outcomes.

Step 5: Review the personal action plan with cross-functional peers. Groups of cross-functional peers were formed to consider each individual's action plan. Each action plan was displayed on the wall and group members walked around, reading each action plan and giving feedback. The group then discussed three points:

a. Are there any potential synergies in the actions?

b. Are there any conflicts?

c. Do the highest priorities require anyone else to change their action plans?

After the discussion, individuals modified and updated their action plans.

Step 6: Plan the individual's personal alignment. Individuals anticipated the reactions to their action plans from their boss, from peers and from direct reports. They identified specific actions they needed to take to earn the support of these stakeholders.

Step 7: Plan organizational alignment. Cross-functional groups brainstormed ways to get EVERYONE in Pharma involved in aligning their efforts with the strategy. Each group submitted their best recommendation to the Pharma CEO, who in turn discussed the recommendations with the leadership team and chose a few actions to implement.

In the year following this alignment process, the Pharma organization was able to exceed its challenging objectives. The number of projects finalized was greater than expected. Partnerships and alliances increased dramatically. The most critical projects moved forward at unprecedented speed. Pharma was able to deliver these outstanding results because the partners were better aligned to make things happen.

Making Partnership Commitments

Recall that one of the lateral capabilities design tools that Jay Galbraith had in his framework was Lateral Processes, which is two or more organizational units agreeing how they will work together. I have used a tool called the Partnership Commitment to facilitate such agreements.

A Partnership Commitment is a synergistic process that can be used to improve and align any work relationship. It may be used between a manager and/or team and individual performers. It can be an effective tool for aligning your organization with its many external stakeholders.

The Partnership Commitment provides a framework for agreement and commitment to perform in four crucial areas:

1. **RESULTS:** specifies *what* outputs are to be delivered by *when* and *why*. These outputs may be listed as:

- Business results
- Service levels
- Financial targets
- Deadlines and timetable milestones
- Connection to mission, vision, values, strategy, goals and priorities…
- The *why* is defined by the consequences to the organization(s) and the individual(s) for achieving or not achieving the results.

2. **EXPECTATIONS:** *how* the two (or more) partners will work together to deliver the results.

- *Who* is responsible for doing what.
- *How* the Process is defined.
- *Which* values to uphold.
- The other do's and don'ts that define the relationship.

3. **RESOURCES:** the tools and people required to deliver the results.

- Budget
- Staffing levels
- Specific team members
- Facilities
- Equipment
- Time commitments

4. **MONITORING:** The agreed-upon timing and methodology for tracking progress towards the results. One question the partners need to answer is, "How long can we let things go

before making sure that everything is on track?" Monitoring includes:

- Agreement on the reporting cycle (daily, weekly, monthly, quarterly, etc.).
- Agreement on the metrics (how will we measure the results?)
- Agreement on data to be gathered (stakeholder feedback, financial data, qualitative measures, other).

On the surface, the Partnership Commitment appears to be a simple thing. These four elements are just *common sense*, you might say, but most of my clients say the Partnership Commitment is not common practice.

Here is an example of a real Partnership Commitment crafted between the Shell Oil Company and one of its contractors:

Some years ago, Shell spent $30-50 million each year on new and replacement oil tanks. Chicago Bridge and Iron (CBI), one of Shell's largest contractors, approached Shell with a proposal to create a partnership that would provide more of a win for both corporations. CBI told its Shell customers, "You bid out all of your tank work each year, but we always get about 75 percent of the contracts. Would you be interested in really partnering with us?" The Shell managers were interested, but just a little skeptical. What did CBI mean by "really partnering?" CBI wanted 100 percent of Shell's business! "Put all our eggs in one basket?" the Shell managers asked themselves. They cautiously agreed to discuss the subject further.

Representatives of the two companies held three meetings in which they shared the principles and practices of how each liked to do business. They particularly focused on how each worked with its customers and suppliers. They also discussed their technical standards for designing and constructing oil tanks. They found their values, technical standards, and competencies were closely aligned.

The partners on both sides decided they were ready to craft a Partnership Commitment, recognizing they would both have to abandon some past assumptions and practices and do some things differently in the future.

CBI and Shell each dedicated one manager exclusively to their partnered account. The first thing they tackled was the job bidding process. It was viewed as time consuming, costly, and not very effective. An oil tank proposal, for example, might go through a full engineering review four or five times: once by each prospective vendor and once by Shell. Shell paid for each of these reviews. The partners agreed that CBI alone would do all of these reviews in the future. This decision alone saved Shell $1 million per year!

Then CBI told Shell, "Instead of telling us the dimensions and materials you want to use in your tank, just tell us how much gas you want to store. Let us come back to you with the best way to do a quality job at the lowest possible price." That sounded good to the Shell managers, but how could they be sure we would be getting the best deal in the current market? CBI volunteered to open its books and scope the project in detail as if they were bidding on the open market.

Here's a summary of the Partnership Commitment Shell and CBI agreed to:

RESULTS

- Store the desired volume of gas at the lowest possible price
- Quality, reliable storage facilities
- A target lump sum total cost
- A win-win profit margin

EXPECTATIONS

- Shell no longer specifies dimensions and materials to be used.
- CBI opens its books and scopes the project in detail as if it were bidding on the open market.

- CBI removes any contingency provisions in its bid.

RESOURCES

- CBI and Shell both dedicate one manager exclusively to the partnership.
- CBI alone does the engineering review of the project.

MONITORING

- A joint steering team meets quarterly to review the results.
- Any deviation in profits or total costs (+ or -) to be split 50-50 between CBI and Shell.

After the first year of operating by the Partnership Commitment, Shell had saved $9 million from its annual budget ($42 million) for tanks. And CBI had increased its Shell business by 25 percent.

Think of the potential wins you and your external stakeholders might achieve with such commitments in the future: breakthroughs in media alliances, in trade agreements, in legal contracts, in research, in production reliability, in quality, in cycle times. As you can see, the real contribution of the Partnership Commitment is that it helps you and your partners shape your new relationship so that both of you come out ahead.

Mobilizing to Help Each Other in Tough Times

One final principle related to synergistic partnerships is one that really can't be designed per se. It emerges naturally as a result of the other synergistic partnership principles. It is the exact opposite of this experience one of my clients had:

"I worked once for a supervisor who was the antithesis of what you read about in all the leadership books. He was demanding, unforgiving and always wanted more from us. He had no time for our personal dilemmas or needs. If we wanted to keep our jobs, we would be at work. It was as simple as that.

"One day, at the end of the shift on a Friday afternoon, he came to each one of us and asked if we could stay another hour or two as a favor to him. He wasn't authorized to pay overtime and he couldn't force us to stay. But he was in a fix and he was asking us if we could help him out just this once....Every one of us politely told him we couldn't stay any longer. We put on our coats and walked out of the factory, leaving him to solve his own problem."

In contrast to this situation, those who truly develop synergistic partnerships become aware of a wider range of stakeholder needs and mobilize themselves and their company's resources when they see others are going through some tough times. Such situations can't be scripted; they reveal how deep one's partnership values really are. For instance:

In the days following the September 11, 2001 destruction of the World Trade Center in New York City, a major concert was organized to raise donations for the victims and their families. Musical stars including Celine Dion and Bruce Springsteen donated their talents for the concert so that all proceeds would go to these individuals. Two days before the concert, the company responsible for handling the telephone donation process announced to the concert organizers it would be unable to do the job. The task was too overwhelming, time was too short, and not enough people had agreed to work overtime, the company said. In desperation, the concert organizers approached the Capital One Financial Corporation about the possibility of handling the phone transactions. CEO Richard Fairbank and President Nigel Morris put out an email message, asking if there would be any volunteers interested in helping out (and putting everything else in their lives on hold for 48 hours). Within hours they had more than 7,000 volunteers (approximately 40 percent of its U.S. workforce). Together they swiftly and efficiently organized the transaction process and handled more than 300,000 calls during the concert, which brought in more than $150 million in donations.

One company responds to the concert crisis by taking a seat on the sidelines. Capital One responds by taking action. Capital One advertises one of its strengths is helping customers with issues that others can't touch. It hires people, in part, who like to be involved in community service. Then, with these subtle factors in place, Capital One spontaneously mobilizes to help some partners when a crisis erupts.

Another example of helping partners in troubled times comes from the Honda Motor Company's Ohio operations. The Honda corporate philosophy is to build life-long supplier relationships. Honda, however, goes beyond the contractual partnership. It has staff resources exclusively dedicated to helping suppliers with problems in quality, engineering or operations. When one supplier was overwhelmed by a dramatic growth in its business, Honda sent a small team to work with the supplier full time for nine months to get on top of the situation.

Why does Honda invest so heavily in its suppliers' well-being? Because they value partnering. They know their success is intertwined with their suppliers' success. They have associates whose daily priorities are aligned with suppliers' priorities so, when they see a partner's unforeseen dilemma, Honda people mobilize their resources to help.

Some companies find that synergistic partnerships can be forged even if there has been little, if any, prior business relationship. You can win a new partner's help in your hour of need.

Tom, the General Counsel for a large consumer products company, was also the industry representative for those who sold products in steel aerosol cans. One of the industry's dilemmas was how to dispose of these cans and recycle them. Waste disposal companies weren't interested in being responsible for smashing the cans and thereby releasing fluorocarbons that could damage the earth's ozone layer. Tom was asked by the industry council to see if he could find someone willing to do the recycling.

Reviewing some of the principles outlined in this chapter, Tom went to see the CEO of a large waste disposal company. As he entered the CEO's office, Tom introduced his purpose by saying, "I'm here on behalf of the aerosol can industry to see if we can find a win-win way to work together to recycle these cans. First off, let me say that I will not ask you to do anything you don't feel is right. I am hopeful we might find a way to recycle these cans and address any concerns you have. But if we can't, we can't."

The CEO responded with deeply-felt concerns about the safety risk to his associates by being exposed to exploding cans as they were crushed. He also mentioned the controversy of releasing the fluorocarbons into the ozone layer and didn't want any part of that. Tom summarized, "So if we can't find a way to protect your workers from the safety hazard and prevent the fluorocarbons from being released, there is no point in talking further." The CEO heartily agreed.

Then Tom invited the CEO to partner with him to find some ways to (1) recycle the cans by a process that (2) would not endanger waste disposal associates and (3) would not release the fluorocarbons into the atmosphere. Because Tom had been so clear in setting a goal for mutual success, the CEO trusted that more conversation might be worthwhile. And indeed it was, as the two eventually defined a process that met all three criteria. The new partnership significantly increased the revenues of the waste disposal company and saved those in the aerosol can industry $40 million annually.

Synergistic Partnerships and Survival

The examples in this chapter show that synergistic partnerships are not ivory tower, pie-in-the-sky clichés. Rather, they are business relationships that can far outperform those who can rely only on contractual transactions.

Those who are "partner beings" find, as Terry Warner stated in the quote at the beginning of this chapter, that "allegiance flow[s] without expense of energy on their part."

Partners who are truly committed to each other's success learn, as Walmart, Procter & Gamble and Saturn did, that the partnership can achieve more than they dreamed.

Companies who pay the price to align individual priorities with the stakeholder ecosystem around them experience how many typical barriers disappear. The work flows freely forward as it did for the Pharma organization.

Stakeholders who define and work according to a Partnership Commitment, like Shell and Chicago Bridge & Iron did, receive a high return on investment, and, with all of the other Survival Code principles kicking in, some synergies will emerge when you least expect them, such as in the cases of Capital One, suppliers to Honda, and the aerosol can industry.

Synergistic partnerships can help you survive and even go beyond.

11
Adapting Ad Infinitum

"So we beat on,
boats against the current,
borne back ceaselessly into the past."

—F. SCOTT FITZGERALD, THE GREAT GATSBY

"The only thing more difficult than starting something new
in an organization is stopping something old."

— RUSSELL ACKOFF

"The only two things that people buy are
good feelings and solutions to problems."

—MICHAEL LEBOEUF

"When the winds of change blow,
some build walls,
some build windmills."

—LAO-TSE

The final survival code principle we will examine is adaptation: *re-strategizing and redeploying your resources in the midst of external changes to stay atop the lifecycle.*

In the world of physical science, the second law of thermodynamics states that systems move steadily toward a state of disorganization and death. This is true for many systems, but it is not a governing law for organizations! Organizations are the only living systems that can escape the clutches of the second law of thermodynamics. Organizations can outlive their founders, yet as we saw in the examination of organizational lifecycles, relatively few organizations fulfill this potential. Why do organizations find it so hard to adapt in response to changing market imperatives?

The Organizational Steady State: a Two-Edged Sword

One of the earlier survival code principles is both a blessing and a curse to organizational survival. This is the principle of the steady state: *survival is maintained via steady processes that follow a proven, functional routine.* This steady state allows an organization to expend the energy necessary to fulfill its purpose and also to store up reserves for tough times. An unsteady state may get the results today, but also may consume all the resources, leaving the cupboard bare when an emergency situation arises. So the steady state ensures control limits are observed as this graphic illustrates:

Notice the system's warning signals whenever the process goes beyond the control limits. The steady state forces mobilize to adjust the process and get it back in line. But what if the market shifts dramatically? What if the current purpose with the current steady state no longer fits in the new market?

For example, the steady state graphic might represent SONY at the height of its success with the famous Walkman portable music players. Then Apple introduced its iPod and the whole MP3 revolution transforms the market. What would be SONY's fate if it were to continue manufacturing Walkman players even better than ever before? The product (and perhaps the company itself) would begin the descent down the lifecycle. In fact, here is what the graphic would look like in this situation:

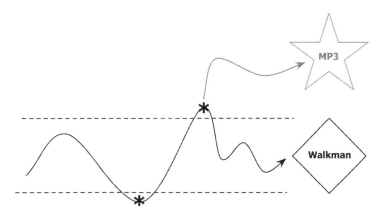

Attempts by SONY associates to manufacture MP3s would be treated *by the system* as a deviation, something to be corrected and brought back within the acceptable limits. You are familiar with the many statements that people use to defend the steady state against a new intrusion:

- "That new invention is a fad. It won't last."
- "We need to do a better job of marketing to show consumers why our product is still better."
- "The new gizmo might get a small market share, but it won't hurt us."
- "It is not realistic to expect us to scrap all of our existing technology and start all over again."
- "We can hold our market share with lower pricing."

This kind of thinking then produces actions that protect today's steady state: dropping prices for horse carriages, adding more jewels to mechanical (vs. quartz movement) timepieces, offering combo meal packages for unhealthy foods and producing more powerful TV antennas.

Systems Require Two Types of Feedback

In the world of cybernetics (the study of regulatory systems) there are two different types of feedback that help a living system survive over time:

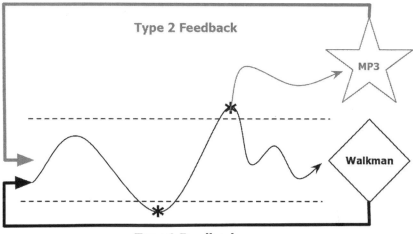

Type 1 Feedback

Type 1 feedback measures deviation from the purpose and steady state and Type 2 feedback tells the system it must deviate from the steady state; that the target has moved. Organizations usually do better at Type 1 feedback than Type 2. Kodak is an example of a problem with Type 2 feedback as it has clung to its photographic film heritage and resisted for years those signals that indicated the digital age was overtaking its industry. Just think about the real world implications of the steady state's strong forces that are actually working against corporate survival:

- Federal mail services go on as usual as they are being replaced by services provided by Federal Express, United Parcel Service and the Internet.
- Companies manufacture paper diaries and planners though many view them as a poor substitute for what one can do with a smart phone or electronic tablet.

- Videotapes and DVDs struggle for life while being made obsolete by Internet streaming services.
- Newspapers fight for subscribers against the tide of individuals getting the same news faster and cheaper via the Internet.

To survive such marketplace turbulence, companies today must become better at studying what is happening in the outside world and planning appropriate responses. The appropriate response to external changes that redefine the system's target is to redesign the operational parameters.

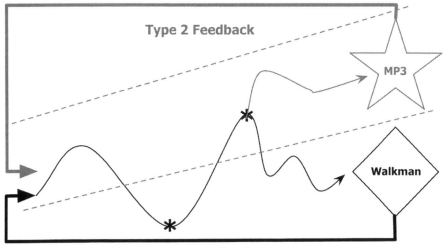

Notice in this graphic how the steady state's control limits have shifted to align with the new target. The organization has now adapted itself to emerging market needs.

Stora Enso: The World's Oldest Industrial Company

Stora Enso is generally regarded as the oldest industrial company in the world.[4] It is a great example of a business enterprise that has adapted successfully to changing world conditions.

A document in 1288 first mentioned the existence of Stora Kopperberg, a Swedish copper mining enterprise operating under the direction of the Swedish crown, nobility, and foreign merchants. In medieval times, this company supplied copper for many purposes, most notably the construction of ships and cathedral steeples throughout Europe. Stora was a major contributor to the Swedish economy.

Through the centuries as technology and lifestyles evolved, Stora's business has adapted successfully from mining to pulp and paper manufacturing and wood products today.

It merged with Finland's Enso Oyj in 1998 and today is the world's second largest pulp and paper manufacturer. Through each of its adaptive phases, Stora Enso has revised its purpose, established a steady state to produce new products, mobilized resources, developed complex skills in new businesses and synergized with new partners to enable it to stay on top. Stora's 13th century copper mines have long since exhausted their resources, but the company lives on, with 30,000 associates in 85 units on all continents still making a significant contribution to the quality of life for many of us.

---

4   Sweden: The oldest corporation in the world, *Time Magazine,* March 15, 1963.

How to Jump the Curve

Let's consider how your company can jump the lifecycle curve as Stora Enso did. First, we need to review the lifecycle dynamics through the lens of adaptation.

This illustration of the S-Curve connects the Organizational Survival Code principles with the rise of organizational performance. Some companies go through this process once and then travel onward for years with very little adaptation. Organization design, to such company leaders, is a process to be used in a crisis, or when they desire a new strategy. Thereafter, they reason, you just have to use good management to handle what comes your way.

Good management, if not aligned with the survival code, will not be sufficient, as evidenced by the number of Global 100 companies that move out of their leadership positions and by the number of companies and brands that disappear through the years. As the graphic shows, if you want your company to jump the curve, you have to start at the beginning of the survival code and do it all over again when market conditions require it.

Organizing for Adaptation

One reason organizations find adaptation difficult, is that no one's explicitly responsible for it. Certainly CEOs and other senior officers should be keeping an eye on such things, but it is easy to lose sight of the need for adaptation when the demands of the here-and-now operation and steady state are almost overwhelming. Remember the discussion in Chapter 7 about criteria for placing boundaries in work processes. The time element is one justification for a boundary. Keeping proper attention to long-term issues often requires a separation from those who are addressing short-term issues. Thus, one of the first issues to tackle is how to organize the tasks of the adaptation process.

Some companies assign specific individuals to monitor the external world and provide analysis and recommendations for action. Many companies find that such attention is needed in several dimensions: marketing, consumer research, market economics, product/service technology, operations, legal and others. These specialists are often formed into a team or teams to collaborate and synergize their insights and recommendations. As one example of this, Procter & Gamble has two separate product development teams for each of its big brands, such as Charmin toilet tissue. One team manages the current Charmin product in the market. At the same time a different team is working on the development of the Charmin product you won't see for another five years. This is one way of building complexity (survival code principle #5) in your organization: the ability to manage today's and tomorrow's business at the same time.

Once you have decided how to structure the work of adaptation, what should the different players actually do? The following sections suggest approaches to this question.

Adapting to Fit into the Ecological Order

The task here is to have consistent monitoring of the two types of feedback:

1. Monitoring your performance vs. strategy.
2. Monitoring the need to change the strategy itself.

Some of the tools we have already reviewed can be helpful in delivering both types of feedback. A stakeholder feedback system, a balanced scorecard, benchmarking and monitoring of business results all are helpful in keeping you on track to fulfill your strategy. Additionally, those responsible for adaptation can also review these feedback data for insights and implications for the need to adapt.

Certainly there are other specific Type 2 feedback inputs that your particular organization might need. Those looking for Type 2 could supplement other feedback data by including non-customers as well as customers. Here is one example from a colleague:

Ann had recently purchased a new compact car and received a phone call from an associate in the factory that had made her car. The associate asked Ann a series of questions about the quality of her vehicle and how satisfied she was overall with her purchase. She was also asked for any ideas she had on how the car could be improved.

A few days later she received a call from an associate of the Honda Motor Company. "Mrs. Green," the caller said, "some weeks ago you test drove a Honda, but did not buy it. Have you purchased a new car recently?"

"Yes," Ann replied.

"Would you mind if I asked you a few questions about your experiences driving the Honda and driving your new car?"

Ann was then asked what it was she liked about her new car, much along the lines of her first phone call from her car's manufacturer. Then she was asked what she did and did not like about driving the Honda. Finally, she was asked what led her to choose her new car over the Honda.

The Honda research is a good example of gathering Type 2 feedback: finding out what all key stakeholders in your industry really need, not just what your current customers think of your existing products. What if Kodak or SONY had gathered such feedback in the early days of the transformation of their industries? What could your company learn if it did such research today?

Regardless of the specific feedback your company may need, the bottom line in this area is to have individuals specifically charged to look regularly at both Type 1 and Type 2 feedback sources to monitor how well your enterprise fits into the stakeholder ecosystem today and in the future.

Adapting Your Strategy

Growing out of the previous section is the need to take a focused look at your strategy in light of feedback and recommendations you might get. In Chapter 5, I referred to this dynamic as Strategy Check.

Effective feedback will tell you what needs and possibilities exist in the market. Prioritizing those needs and possibilities and focusing future efforts is the work of strategy. What might make your current strategy, products or services obsolete?

What opportunities could you exploit to strengthen your future business?

One consideration in adapting your strategy is the framework articulated by economist Joseph Schumpeter as the market dynamics of Technology push vs. Market pull.

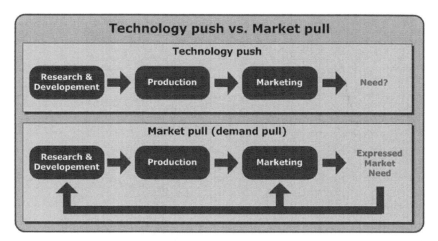

Market pull refers to the dynamic of discovering a customer's need and then organizing research & development, production and marketing efforts to meet that need. The evolution from home music systems to the MP3 is a good example of this. Research indicated people wanted to be able to listen to their music away from home. Car stereos fulfilled part of this need, SONY's Walkman expanded on this fulfillment, and MP3s have gone beyond all others to enable people to listen in their cars, while walking or even while doing strenuous athletic activities–all with the same player. Today, you see MP3s everywhere you go.

Technology push is a different dynamic. This describes a company using its know-how to create a new product that no customer has asked for. No one asked for a disposable diaper until Procter & Gamble introduced Pampers. P&G researchers had gained expertise in absorbent materials by making toilet tissue and paper towels. Someone proposed that the same need might exist for diaper products. This led to the introduction of Pampers and, in just a few short years, disposable diapers became THE way of diapering babies in many lands. Similarly, no customers were asking for a Post It Note. A legendary 3M researcher working on adhesive formulas stumbled across an adhesive that would bond, release and bond again. He postulated that many people would have a need for such an adhesive for notes. No one asked for it, but a grateful public now uses Post It Notes in all sizes from thumbnails to wall posters.

As you examine your strategy, Schumpeter's framework gives you two good questions to ask:

- What customer needs could we fulfill better than anyone else?
- What products or services could we provide with our skills and technology that no one is asking for, but we know would win an immediate following?

As you canvass the marketplace to learn how fit your strategy is, also keep in mind the historical factors that have moved companies up and down the Global 100 list:

- New technology: How is this affecting us? What are the threats? The opportunities?
- Changing economics: How will our products and services fare in the emerging global financial market? What are the imperatives for quality, cost and value?
- Mergers: Are there potential partners out there that could enhance our market position? Are there players out there with whom we definitely do not want to join?

Adapting Your Work Processes

We have seen the example of Stora Enso in adapting its product lines to include entirely new businesses. Copper mining requires different know-how from that of pulp and paper manufacturing. In such transitions, it is important to remember the need to design quality processes that can go head to head successfully with established industry leaders or other new entrants in the category. All of the design features we have discussed about free-flowing processes, minimizing handoffs, solving problems at their source and building self-sufficiency apply to new lines of business as well.

Steve Jobs and Steve Wozniak did their homework before attempting to start up Apple Computer. They partnered with a number of industry experts and studied what other computer companies did to arrive at their production models. From the very beginning, Apple has had state-of-the art processes and equipment to deliver its products, and those processes have been adapted through the years as the computers evolved and additional products like the iPod, iPhone and iPad have been released.

The competitive market doesn't care whether you are new or an experienced hand in an industry. If you try to compete with inferior processes, even the best of products will suffer. If your adaptation requires delivering new products or services, you will need to pay the price in process design to be competitive from the first day in the new business.

Adapting Your Level of Complexity

The adaptation process must also address the survival code principle of complexity. New skills may need to be infused into your organization. New work processes may require different combinations of skills. Individuals and organizational units may need to learn new things to function self-sufficiently in the new processes and team structures may also need to be altered. Here are some questions to consider in adapting to the new requirements for complexity:

- What skills do we need to develop in our associates? Who needs those skills?
- What skills do we need to get from our partners? Do we need a temporary infusion of technical skills, or marketing skills, or strategic analysis skills? Is the need just for the startup/transition period or is this an ongoing need?
- What skills and expertise do we need to buy from outside experts, other companies, etc.?

- In what ways can we utilize our current competencies in new arenas?
- What skill mix and resources do the new organizational units require to be self-sufficient in the daily operation?

Adapting Your Partner Relationships

James Brian Quinn, Professor Emeritus at Dartmouth University, likes to say, "If you aren't the best in the world at something, you are giving up competitive advantage by doing it yourself." This challenging statement raises some important issues related to adaptation and survival. As your corporation moves forward to adapt to new economics, new technologies, new markets and cultures, and new products and services, just how much capacity for adaptation should you expect from your existing resources? Should everyone have to reinvent themselves in every dimension? Or should you take advantage of partnering with others who are already strong in areas you need to master? Some questions, similar to those raised in the previous section, include:

- Would we be better off partnering with someone else to get the needed skills to win in today's (tomorrow's) marketplace?
- How can we turn key stakeholder relationships from transactional ones to true partnerships like Saturn did?
- How can we learn from those who excel today at what we are going to be doing in the future?

Ritz-Carlton began shaping its gold standard of service by having executives attend Walt Disney University. Disney, still a model organization for customer service, imparted its experiences and standards to Ritz-Carlton, who customized the Disney formula to fit their hotel business. Procter & Gamble learned organizational principles from universities and other corporations to develop its "technician concept" for manufacturing team-based systems in the late '60s. Research divisions in many corporations have partnered for years with scientists on university faculties to spearhead new breakthroughs in medicine, engineering and the hard sciences. Many global competitors partner with local marketing experts to understand a local market and social culture before moving into a new geography.

As these examples show, partnering in today's complex world can yield faster, less expensive, and ultimately more effective solutions for your enterprise than trying to master everything with your current staff. Analyze thoroughly how you must adapt to the new market demands. Choose carefully the partnerships that will help keep you on the top of the lifecycle. Then remember, calling each other a partner doesn't make it so. The magic starts when you both start *being* partners.

Adapting What You Inherited to Shape Your Legacy

In previous chapters, we have reviewed how companies like Ritz-Carlton, Procter & Gamble, General Electric, Walmart, US

Synthetic, Apple, Honda, Shell, and many others have designed their organizations according to the Organizational Survival Code and have reaped the benefits. The leaders in each of these companies inherited different levels of performance, cultural strengths, liabilities, and strategies. They also have inherited rapidly-changing market dynamics due to economic setbacks, more sophisticated global competition, new technologies and changing customer needs. The leaders whose accomplishments we admire and whose products and services we buy today all have taken what they inherited from their predecessors and reshaped their companies to stay on top amidst all the changes. Their legacy is not measured in quarterly earnings or annual dividends alone. Their true legacy is that their companies are still formidable contestants in the competitive race.

The capacity for adaption is at the heart of corporate survival. This capacity requires putting to use all of the other survival code principles. To survive, you must:

- Fit into the evolving order of your key stakeholders' needs.
- Shape (and reshape) a strategy that is so compelling that associates instinctively act to fulfill it.
- Design high quality processes that become an effective steady state.
- Mobilize to do whatever it takes to ensure stakeholder needs are met.
- Develop the complex set of skills and self-sufficiency so that individuals and units can see to the system's survival needs.

- Become synergistic partners with key stakeholders to exceed what each could deliver alone.
- Constantly measure what you are delivering vs. changing market needs and begin again with step one of the survival code as the market requires.

These seven principles are not hard to understand, but are not always easy to put into practice. The leaders who have succeeded by adherence to these principles are not superhuman in their managerial skills, but they do have a commitment to learn and to do whatever it takes to survive in tough times.

In the concluding chapter, we will explore an even greater legacy forged by these leaders and organizations.

PART THREE:
Beyond Survival

12
Meaningful Contributions Endure

"When all is said and done this business is nothing but a symbol and when we translate this we find that it means a great many people think well of its products and that a great multitude has faith in the integrity of the people who make this product. In a very short time the machines that are now so lively will soon become obsolete and the big buildings for all their solidity must someday be replaced. But a business which symbolizes can live so long as there are human beings alive, for it is not built of such flimsy materials as steel and concrete, it is built of human opinions which may be made to live forever. The goodwill of the people is the only enduring thing in any business. It is the sole substance...The rest is shadow!"

—HERBERT FISK JOHNSON, SR.

"I dread...lest [people] should at last so entirely give way to a cowardly love of present enjoyment, as to lose sight of interests

of future selves and those of their descendants; and prefer to glide along the easy current of life, rather than make, when it is necessary, a strong and sudden effort to higher purpose.

—ALEXIS DE TOCQUEVILLE

Dot was a Georgia native and a happily married housewife with a strong family, when her husband suffered a debilitating heart attack and was no longer able to work. Suddenly, Dot became the provider for her family. She was hired as a technician at a Procter & Gamble Pampers operation in Albany, Georgia. The P&G plant was pioneering several design approaches discussed in this book. One of these approaches was a pay system that better rewarded technicians for their contributions to plant success. Dot learned to operate all production equipment, learned skills in some support functions and eventually became her team's production coordinator. Because of this mix of skills and her team's outstanding production results (one of the best in the entire company), Dot earned the plant's top pay level. Her standard of living was higher than ever before.

Frank was a frequent business traveler who often spent weeks at a time away from home and family. Through the means provided by social media (Email, Skype, Facebook and Twitter) and a smartphone with a built-in camera, Frank has been able to communicate frequently and occasionally even "live" with his wife, children, parents and siblings. Frank is now "there" to plan family business with his wife even when he is thousands of miles away. He is "there" to hear his child rehearse a big school presentation. He is "there" to wish his mother a happy birthday. "I have a much stronger connection to my family now when I am on the road," Frank said. "Thank goodness for modern technology."

Founders Don and Deyon Stephens of Mercy Ships have turned dreams and prayers into reality by delivering health care services to those who could never afford them. Since 1978 Mercy Ships has performed services valued at more than $834 million and treated over 2.9 million people with over 563 port visits in 53 developing nations and 17 developed nations. The organization depends totally on donations for its survival. There have been many points of financial hardship in its history, but Mercy Ships associates and their sponsors have always found a way to keep their ship afloat. Their mission is truly life changing—for both the providers and the patients.

The hidden thread connecting these three examples is the shared quest by Procter & Gamble, Facebook, Twitter, Microsoft, Apple and Mercy Ships to survive in a rapidly changing marketplace. Ironically, as these companies developed survival skills through more competitive products and services, they also improved the lives of their stakeholders.

Survive and Thrive in Difficult Times

The collateral benefit to those organizations that adapt and stay at the top of their game is that they don't merely survive;

they often thrive, advancing the quality of life for themselves and their many stakeholders.

We see this phenomenon everywhere in today's marketplace. A laundry product that jumps the curve is a *better product* than its predecessor. A hybrid car gets superior gas mileage to conventional models. Today's farming methods deliver more food at less cost to consumers in a wide variety of climates and growing conditions. Modern medical science can prolong life and enable self-sufficiency far beyond what our ancestors could have imagined. The ever-advancing computer technology enables us to learn more things faster, be virtually present everywhere, and be more productive in our work.

In short, adherence to the Survival Code actually moves us beyond mere survival.

Beyond Work to Contribution

Occasionally, I have come in contact with individuals who believe that all companies are exploitive, self-serving, and wasteful. Indeed, some companies are guilty of these things, but how many companies are contributing today to our excellent standard of living? I maintain that another key intangible in organizational performance is the degree to which individuals can see how their contributions really do raise the quality of life for many people.

McDonnell Douglas CEO Harry Stonecipher had a great desire to make clear to his associates who actually assembled MD aircraft how much more meaningful their contribution was than just installing rivets or putting together a landing wheel assembly. He mobilized creative resources to begin a campaign, first via posters in the assembly facilities and then through TV advertising spots, to show the deep significance of McDonnell Douglas' contribution to the world.

One of these messages showed several school children looking out the window of their school bus. The caption read: "One of these kids will fly to space. One will fly to defend our freedom. One will fly hope to a land where there is none. Who will fly with them? McDonnell Douglas will."

Take a moment and think about the big picture of your own work. Think of the work you do and the products and services that your company provides. Don't just think about what you *produce*. Think about what you *contribute* to our society. This will elevate your appreciation and value for what you do.

The Incredible Saga of John Crowley

One poignant example of the difference between merely doing your work and making a contribution is the experience of John and Aileen Crowley. Their life was changed forever on the day in 1998 when the doctors told them that their daughter Megan had Pompe disease, a rare illness that attacks the muscles and nerves and is fatal to those who have it, especially young children. The Crowleys' third child, Patrick, was born a few days later and also was diagnosed with Pompe.

The Crowleys' quest to find a cure for their children has been chronicled in several books, periodicals, the film *Extraordinary Measures*, and a Harvard Business School case study. As John began organizing resources to find a cure for Pompe, he was led to Dr. William Canfield, who was working on an enzyme replacement therapy to treat the disease. After some years of development work, they concluded they needed deeper financial pockets and eventually sold their company to Genzyme, the third largest biotech company in the world. Crowley was placed in charge of all Pompe research that included Canfield's work plus similar research on enzyme replacement compounds that was already underway at Genzyme.

John observed there were four separate research teams working on possible cures for Pompe, but the four never communicated with each other. His initial efforts to build faster learning and collaboration among the teams were rebuffed by Genzyme's corporate culture. "That's not the way we do things around here," he was told. "Each team takes an entrepreneurial approach. It builds great ownership for the outcome."

As head of the overall research, John did two things that made a big difference. First he invited parents and their children who had Pompe to attend a meeting with everyone who was working on the four projects. Many of Genzyme's employees had never met a person with the disease. This experience helped everyone see that tasks, studies and tests were only trivial stepping stones toward the real goal: a life-saving contribution that so many desperately awaited.

With everyone now focused on contribution rather than tasks alone, John successfully established a leadership council with representation of all four teams. The council came together to share learning, research findings and hypotheses for the ultimate treatment. In due time, one solution emerged and was submitted to the FDA for approval.

In January 2003, Megan and Patrick Crowley received their first treatment of Myozyme, a mere five years after Megan's initial diagnosis. (In the pharmaceutical world, it is not unusual for drug development to take 10 years or more for final release.) Myozyme cannot cure Pompe, but arrests its life-threatening effects on the body with regular dosage. John's leadership helped everyone at Genzyme operate according to the survival code to save his own (and many other) children's lives. What a great contribution they all have made! What success naturally came forth from a compelling purpose, collaborative structures, and sound medical research.

Contribution Is the Real Bottom Line

Experiences like those at Genzyme reveal the true potential of human organizations. Machines are systems, but they just sit there. Animals are living systems, but most of the time they only respond to their environment. A human organization may cycle up and down like a machine, or it may merely respond to its environment like an animal. It is only by tapping into that part of us that is uniquely human that we can make a contribution that no other system can make. We, the programmers of our organizations, can dream, put real purpose into our work, and organize our resources to get the results we really want and need. As former Ritz-Carlton president Horst Schulze says, "A chair fulfills a function; people need a purpose. *It is immoral to ask people to work without purpose.*"

The noblest purpose for organizations, one that enables them to survive and thrive even in the toughest of times, is to make significant contributions to society's quality of life. This builds, in the words of Herbert Fisk Johnson, "the goodwill of the people...*the only enduring thing in any business...The rest is shadow!"*

Winston Churchill once said, "To everyone there comes in their lifetime that special moment when they are figuratively tapped on the shoulder and offered the chance to do a very special thing, unique to them and fitted to their talent; what a tragedy if that moment finds them unprepared or unqualified for the work which would be their finest hour."

It is my hope that reading this book has prepared and will qualify you for that work which will become your finest hour. May you and your colleagues survive–and thrive–in the days and years ahead.

About The Author

David Hanna is a principal with the RBL Group, a firm of thought leaders, consultants, and former executives dedicated to helping clients create results that deliver sustainable value. Previously he was an internal consultant with Procter & Gamble and an external consultant and program leader with Franklin Covey and the Confluence Group. He has worked with Top 500 companies all over the world. His areas of expertise include leadership development, organization diagnosis, high performance work design, executive coaching, team development and change management. He is the author of two other books: *Designing Organizations for High Performance* (Addison-Wesley, 1988), listed as one of the Great Business Books by Maven House Press, and *Leadership for the Ages* (Executive Excellence Publishing, 2001). Dave received his B.A. in Communications and his M.A. in Organizational Behavior from Brigham Young University.